REPORT

Health Benefits for Medicare-Eligible Military Retirees

Rationalizing TRICARE for Life

Michael Schoenbaum, Barbara Wynn,
Terri Tanielian, Katherine Harris,
Renee Labor, C. Ross Anthony

Prepared for the Office of the Secretary of Defense

NATIONAL DEFENSE RESEARCH INSTITUTE and
RAND HEALTH

The research described in this report was sponsored by the Office of the Secretary of Defense (OSD). The research was conducted jointly by RAND Health and the RAND National Defense Research Institute, a federally funded research and development center supported by the OSD, the Joint Staff, the unified commands, and the defense agencies under Contract DASW01-01-C-0004.

Library of Congress Cataloging-in-Publication Data

Health benefits for medicare-eligible military retirees : rationalizing TRICARE for life / Michael Schoenbaum ... [et al.].
   p. cm.
   "TR-118."
   Includes bibliographical references.
   ISBN 0-8330-3649-1 (pbk. : alk. paper)
   1. Retired military personnel—Medical care—United States. 2. Medicare. 3. Health maintenance organizations—United States. 4. Managed care plans (Medical care)—United States. 5. United States. Dept. of Defense—Rules and practice. 6. United States. Office of the Assistant Secretary of Defense (Health Affairs). TRICARE Management Activity. I. Schoenbaum, Michael.

UB449.H43 2004
368.4'26'0086970973—dc22

2004017571

The RAND Corporation is a nonprofit research organization providing objective analysis and effective solutions that address the challenges facing the public and private sectors around the world. RAND's publications do not necessarily reflect the opinions of its research clients and sponsors.

RAND® is a registered trademark.

Published 2004 by the RAND Corporation
1700 Main Street, P.O. Box 2138, Santa Monica, CA 90407-2138
1200 South Hayes Street, Arlington, VA 22202-5050
201 North Craig Street, Suite 202, Pittsburgh, PA 15213-1516
RAND URL: http://www.rand.org/
To order RAND documents or to obtain additional information, contact
Distribution Services: Telephone: (310) 451-7002;
Fax: (310) 451-6915; Email: order@rand.org

Preface

The 2001 National Defense Authorization Act expanded eligibility for TRICARE coverage to Medicare-eligible military retirees age 65 or over. Effective October 1, 2001, Medicare-eligible military retirees enrolled in Medicare Part B became entitled to both Medicare and TRICARE health care benefits. This coverage is referred to as TRICARE for Life (TFL). Under this program, Medicare is the primary payer and TRICARE the secondary payer for Medicare-covered services. In addition, TRICARE covers all Medicare cost-sharing by patients, including Medicare deductibles and coinsurance. Regular TRICARE benefits apply to services that Medicare does not cover.

This report examines the TFL legislation and its implementation. The authors summarize issues and policy options that were discussed in several briefings presented to the Department of Defense (DoD) for its consideration of options for improving TFL in the future. This report is not intended to be a complete discussion of TRICARE or Medicare benefits. Rather, its aim is to provide an overview of TFL and to highlight certain issues for further consideration, in particular those that may pose potential policy and/or implementation difficulties for DoD.

The findings and recommendations reported here are based primarily on information gathered between June and September 2001, prior to TFL implementation. DoD considered many of the issues discussed in this report during the TFL implementation process, and some of the authors' recommendations have been implemented or are still under active review as of this writing. Because this report was prepared after the TFL implementation, the authors note those issues identified during their research as being problematic, which were then addressed in subsequent legislation. However, they do not consider actual experience under TFL.

This report is directed primarily to policymakers within DoD and in Congress, but it may also be of interest to individuals at the Center for Medicare and Medicaid Services and to other readers interested in health insurance for the DoD/Medicare population.

This research was sponsored by the TRICARE Management Activity under the Assistant Secretary of Defense for Health Affairs. It was carried out jointly by the RAND Health Center for Military Health Policy Research and the Forces and Resources Policy Center of the National Defense Research Institute (NDRI). NDRI is a federally funded research and development center sponsored by the Office of the Secretary of Defense, the Joint Staff, the Unified Commands, and the Defense agencies.

Comments on this report are welcome and may be addressed to the principal investigator, Michael Schoenbaum (mikels@rand.org). For more information on the RAND Corporation Forces and Resources Policy Center, contact the center's director Susan Everingham at susane@rand.org; 310-393-0411, extension 7654; or at the RAND Corporation, 1700

Main Street, Santa Monica, CA 90401. More information about the RAND Corporation is available at www.rand.org.

Contents

Tables

Summary

The National Defense Authorization Act (NDAA) for fiscal year (FY) 2001 made sweeping changes to the way that health care furnished by civilian providers to Medicare-eligible military retirees is financed. The law directed the Department of Defense (DoD) to implement what is now commonly referred to as TRICARE for Life (TFL). As of October 1, 2001, TFL provides TRICARE as supplemental health insurance for all Medicare-eligible military retirees age 65 or older who are enrolled in Medicare Part B. As of 2003, approximately 1.6 million military retirees are eligible for TFL. In general, TRICARE for Life covers all cost-sharing for Medicare-covered services and standard TRICARE cost-sharing for services that are covered by TRICARE but not by Medicare. Thus, TFL provides Medicare-eligible military retirees with one of the most comprehensive health insurance benefit packages in the United States.

Focus of This Study

This study was undertaken in the months preceding implementation of the TFL program. Given the limited time and resources for the study, we focused on three types of issues: those that DoD specifically asked us to examine, those related to services for which Medicare and TRICARE benefits differ significantly, and those of potential operational concern. Our goal was to identify areas that may pose policy and/or implementation problems. Where appropriate, we suggest policy options that DoD might consider in order to accomplish the following:

- Rationalize benefits by considering changes in the TFL benefit structure
- Promote ease of operations by improving compatibility with Medicare benefits
- Improve efficiency by promoting optimal use of direct-care services and limiting excessive liability for civilian care
- Improve the overall benefit package for Medicare-eligible military retirees.

Data and Methodology

We relied on several sources of information in conducting this study. We began with a comprehensive review of relevant policy manuals, literature, and other materials on both the Medicare and TRICARE programs to document and compare the eligibility requirements, benefit definitions, and coverage policies within each program. As appropriate, RAND Corporation staff received copies of internal DoD communications and briefing slides to inform the work. We also conducted a number of formal and informal interviews and discussions with key DoD officials, representatives from each of DoD Surgeons General offices (Army, Navy, and Air Force), and relevant non-DoD experts with regard to particular benefit areas, such as long-term care services.

As stated above, the initial work for this report was done prior to the implementation of TFL. Since the TFL implementation, we have not updated this report to include a discussion of actual experience under TFL or policy changes since TFL implementation; however, we updated our discussion of certain issues, such as post-acute care services and behavioral health issues, that we had originally identified as being problematic and that have been addressed in subsequent legislation. We note those issues, and other issues that remain potentially problematic, in our summary of findings for specific topics.

Benefit and Coverage Policies

Most health care services that are covered benefits under TRICARE are also covered benefits under Medicare, and vice versa. However, because TFL benefits are based on the existing TRICARE program, they were not expressly designed to fit together with Medicare benefits (in contrast to privately purchased Medicare supplemental or "Medigap" policies, which do). As a result, there are benefit and coverage inconsistencies that pose operational challenges and are likely to lead to confusion and misunderstanding for beneficiaries. For example, there are some differences among the providers who can furnish certain services and the settings in which covered services can be provided. Some of these issues should be resolved by Section 705 of the FY2003 NDAA, which provides that a physician or other practitioner who is eligible to receive reimbursement for services under Medicare is also approved to provide care under TFL.

When a service or item is a benefit of both TRICARE and Medicare, TFL relies on Medicare's determinations regarding medical necessity and eligibility for coverage. That is, if a dually covered service claim is denied for reimbursement from Medicare on the basis of lack of medical necessity, TRICARE will not consider the claim for TFL cost-sharing. In cases in which a Medicare claim is denied because it is for a service that is not covered by Medicare, TRICARE will accept the claim for processing and determine whether the item or service is eligible for cost-sharing or payment under current TRICARE policies. If a claim is denied due to lack of medical necessity and is appealable under Medicare, the denial cannot be appealed under TRICARE.

A potential concern for TFL is whether the coding specificity in Medicare's claims determination is sufficient for TRICARE to distinguish between Medicare coverage and medical necessity determinations, establish its cost-sharing liability accurately, and afford the beneficiary sufficient appeal rights. TRICARE Management Activity (TMA)[1] has indicated that the claim denial codes used by the Medicare contractors should be sufficient for TRICARE's purposes, but this hinges on an empirical question that will need to be evaluated in practice.

---

[1] The TMA is an office within the Department of Defense with responsibility for overseeing the administration of health benefits to military dependents and retirees.

Recommendation. Claims for services for which Medicare and TRICARE coverage policies diverge need to be reviewed to assure that the claims adjudication and appeals processes for TFL beneficiaries are working as intended.

We examined in depth three areas that appear to have potentially significant benefit coordination issues: coverage of new and emerging technology, post–acute care services, and behavioral health care services. While legislation subsequent to the TFL implementation improved coordination of benefits between Medicare and TRICARE for post–acute care services and behavioral health services, some potential issues remain, which we discuss in the following subsections.

New and Emerging Technology

Almost by definition, coverage policies for emerging technologies are continuously evolving in both Medicare and TRICARE as new technology is diffused and additional information becomes available on the safety and efficacy of specific technologies. Medicare's coverage policies for a particular technology at a particular point in time may conflict with those that TRICARE has established for beneficiaries under age 65. In addition, Medicare policies may vary geographically by contractor.

We believe that TFL will highlight coverage inconsistencies between TRICARE and Medicare and may create pressure for consistent "federal" coverage policy. As a general rule, there should be a clear rationale for why a certain technology is covered by one program and not the other.

Recommendation. TMA is not represented on the Center for Medicare and Medicaid Services (CMS) Medicare Coverage Advisory Committee (MCAC). Coordination between the two programs could be enhanced if TMA became an active participant in MCAC deliberations. TMA's participation in the committee would create the opportunity for TMA to have input into the coverage determination process and to make deliberate judgments regarding whether TRICARE's coverage policies should deviate from Medicare's.

Behavioral Health Services

Differences in Medicare and TRICARE coverage policies for behavioral health services create complex issues in implementing TFL and make it likely that beneficiaries will find this area of their health coverage relatively confusing. However, benefit administration should be simplified since the elimination of the TRICARE preauthorization requirement for inpatient psychiatric care covered by Medicare Part A benefits, effective October 2003. However, TRICARE has a lifetime limit of three benefit periods for the coverage of substance abuse treatment services, which may remain problematic. Because TRICARE and Medicare define benefit periods differently, the determination of when and how the TRICARE limit is reached is likely to be somewhat complex and confusing to both providers and beneficiaries.

Recommendation. We recommend that DoD consider the impact of removing the three-benefit-period limit on substance abuse benefits for the TFL population. TFL decreases the financial barriers to outpatient mental health services for the dually eligible population and provides few financial incentives to limit care. TFL beneficiaries have unlimited access to medically necessary outpatient psychiatric treatment that will be covered 50 percent by Medicare and 50 percent by TRICARE. In addition, TRICARE provides TFL beneficiaries with pharmacy benefits that lack the limits imposed by standard Medigap plans.

Recommendation. DoD should conduct a close examination of mental health service utilization and costs to determine the impact of providing outpatient mental health care without cost-sharing or benefit limits. This examination should be conducted across the direct- and purchased-care systems.

TFL Beneficiary Cost-Sharing for Civilian Care

TFL is being implemented without premiums, deductibles, or copayments. Compared with the health insurance options previously available to Medicare-eligible military retirees, TFL is likely to be of substantial value to most beneficiaries, with few or no drawbacks. At the same time, TFL will substantially increase federal spending, both because of the new benefits per se and because the absence of cost-sharing is likely to increase health care use by eliminating the incentives that cost-sharing gives beneficiaries to use care efficiently.

DoD and Medicare are likely to benefit if modest cost-sharing is introduced into TFL—for instance, such as the cost-sharing that military retirees under age 65 currently have under TRICARE Prime. Some amount of cost-sharing by beneficiaries is nearly universal in private group health insurance plans, including employer-sponsored retiree plans. For Medicare beneficiaries, supplemental coverage with modest cost-sharing substantially reduces the out-of-pocket costs that would arise under the standard Medicare benefit, while retaining some modest incentives to control health care use and costs.

By "modest" cost-sharing provisions, we envision primarily fixed-dollar copayments, on the order of $10 per visit, for ambulatory care visits. Such copayments are similar in form and magnitude to those required in many employer-sponsored supplemental plans and Medicare+Choice HMOs (and in TRICARE for military retirees under age 65). They are also similar to the copayments currently required under DoD's pharmacy benefit program. Fixed-dollar copayments have the advantage that they are easy to understand and administer; in many private plans, for instance, beneficiaries pay the copayment at the time of service, with no additional required paperwork.

All else being equal, the introduction of cost-sharing in TFL would likely serve to reduce the cost of the program to the federal government. However, this change could be made revenue neutral by applying the resulting savings toward other benefits for the covered population—such as enhanced post-acute or long-term care coverage or a reduction in the current TFL out-of-pocket maximum—thereby potentially increasing the overall value of the TFL benefit.

Recommendation. DoD should evaluate the effect of introducing into TFL modest cost-sharing for civilian care. Further research into the preferences of TFL beneficiaries and the likely consequences of introducing cost-sharing (versus continued free care) in TFL would help identify strategies to maximize the overall value of the TFL benefit.

Managing MTF Care Provided to TFL Beneficiaries

Relatively little opportunity exists to implement managed care practices under standard Medicare and TFL. However, given the apparent desire of many TFL beneficiaries to receive care from military providers, DoD may have the opportunity to provide managed care for some elderly beneficiaries via programs instituted at MTFs, such as TRICARE Plus. Where MTF capacity permits, TRICARE Plus is a primary care enrollment option for military retirees who are not enrolled in a Medicare+Choice plan. It allows some TFL beneficiaries to receive primary care from an MTF on the same priority basis as TRICARE Prime enrollees and to receive specialty care on a space-available basis.

We think it is likely that TRICARE Plus and similar programs will be well received by beneficiaries, especially because participation in them is voluntary. We also think it is plausible that such programs could improve clinical outcomes for some enrollees, relative to both standard Medicare and the current space-available policy. However, the scope of such improvements depends critically on how and for whom care management programs are implemented. DoD may be able to increase the likelihood of improved clinical outcomes by targeting TRICARE Plus enrollment to patients who are likely to benefit from primary care management and implementing effective care management programs for those patients.

Because DoD must assume full responsibility for the cost of care provided to Medicare-eligible beneficiaries at MTFs, DoD's patient care costs are almost certainly higher under TRICARE Plus than the costs of care provided under Medicare. On the other hand, treating Medicare-eligible beneficiaries in MTFs helps DoD to fulfill its readiness mission. How these factors balance on net is unknown.

Recommendation. Further research regarding the effects of MTF primary care management on patient outcomes and treatment costs, and regarding providers' case-mix preferences and the relationship between primary care management and readiness, should be conducted to determine the overall cost-effectiveness of TRICARE Plus from the perspective of DoD and the federal government, relative to alternative models for care management and readiness training.

Models for Medicare Sharing in MTF Costs

DoD's new obligations for TFL beneficiaries raise issues related to the cost of furnishing direct care relative to making secondary payments for civilian care. These new obligations also raise the issue of whether Medicare should share in the costs of direct care services now that the traditional division of responsibilities for military retiree health care costs no longer exists.

Without Medicare cost-sharing for MTF care, DoD costs would be lower if TFL beneficiaries who are currently receiving MTF direct care instead obtain care from civilian providers; however, the shift could negatively affect physician retention and training, create excess capacity at some MTFs, and would run counter to the preferences of many TFL beneficiaries. Moreover, Medicare costs would increase substantially because the program would become the primary payer for civilian care that had previously been furnished by MTFs at no cost to Medicare. Thus, Medicare has an interest in assuring that direct care for TFL beneficiaries continues.

There is an overall federal interest in DoD continuing to provide direct care to TFL beneficiaries, assuming the incremental costs of MTF care are less than the total costs of civilian care. Medicare cost-sharing for MTF care would foster viewing TFL beneficiaries as a joint responsibility of DoD and Medicare and lead to finding ways to provide those beneficiaries with the highest-quality care at the least cost to the federal government. Cost-sharing also would provide DoD with the financial resources to continue to provide direct care to TFL beneficiaries, and it has the potential to meet several policy goals: to give TFL beneficiaries the choice between direct and civilian care, to serve DoD readiness needs, and, most important, to provide high-quality health care services to TFL beneficiaries and the non-retiree military population at the least cost to the federal government. From the perspective of total federal outlays, however, a better understanding of how utilization by TFL beneficiaries who obtain care primarily from MTFs compares with utilization by TFL beneficiaries who obtain care solely through civilian providers is needed before policies are adopted that might encourage future expansion of MTF care for TFL beneficiaries.

Recommendation. Additional research, using a combined Medicare/DoD database for TFL beneficiaries, should be conducted to determine the cost implications of potential cost-sharing options for DoD and the Medicare program and total federal outlays. The research would provide the analyses that are needed to inform a policy discussion regarding appropriate cost-sharing arrangements between Medicare and DoD for TFL beneficiaries. In the end, the question of appropriate cost for direct care is likely to be answered through the political process, which should be supported by good information and analysis.

There are similar cost-sharing issues with the Department of Veterans Affairs (DVA). In keeping with the notion of a "federal program" beneficiary, consideration should be given to expanding the recommended analyses to include veterans who are DoD retirees and/or Medicare beneficiaries and extending the policy discussion to include the DVA.

Acknowledgments

This report reflects the substantial contributions of all six authors. We are grateful to personnel from the TRICARE Management Authority, Military Health System, offices of the Surgeons General of the armed services, and organizations representing military retirees for their participation in the interviews and their willingness to share their views and experiences.

Acronyms

AARP	American Association of Retired People
CFR	Code of Federal Regulations
CHAMPUS	Civilian Health and Medical Program of the Uniformed Service
CMAC	CHAMPUS Maximum Allowable Charge
CMS	Center for Medicare and Medicaid Services
CORF	comprehensive outpatient rehabilitation facility
DEERS	Defense Enrollment Eligibility Reporting System
DHHS	Department of Health and Human Services
DME	durable medical equipment
DoD	Department of Defense
DVA	Department of Veterans Affairs
ESRD	end-stage chronic renal disease
FDA	Food and Drug Administration
FR	*Federal Register*
FY	fiscal year
GAO	U.S. General Accounting Office
HCFA	Health Care Financing Administration
HHA	home health agency
HIE	Health Insurance Experiment
HLA	human leukocyte antigen
HMO	Health Maintenance Organization
H.R.	U.S. House of Representatives
IHS	Indian Health Service
MCAC	Medicare Coverage Advisory Committee
MCSC	Managed Care Support Contractor
MHS	Military Health System
MTF	military treatment facility
NDAA	National Defense Authorization Act

NDRI	National Defense Research Institute
OPT	outpatient physical therapy providers and clinics
PCP	primary care provider
PET	positron emission tomography
PTA	percutaneous transluminal angioplasty
RTC	residential treatment center
S.	U.S. Senate
SNF	skilled nursing facility
TFL	TRICARE for Life
TMA	TRICARE Management Activity
UM	utilization management
U.S.C.	U.S. Code

CHAPTER ONE

Introduction

Overview of TRICARE for Life

The National Defense Authorization Act (NDAA) for fiscal year (FY) 2001[1] made sweeping changes to the way that health care furnished by civilian providers to Medicare-eligible military retirees is financed. The law directed the Department of Defense (DoD) to implement what is now commonly referred to as TRICARE for Life (TFL). As of October 1, 2001, TFL provides TRICARE as supplemental health insurance for all Medicare-eligible military retirees age 65 or older who are enrolled in Medicare Part B. Approximately 1.6 million military retirees are currently eligible for TFL. In general, TRICARE for Life covers all cost-sharing by patients for Medicare-covered services and covers standard TRICARE cost-sharing by patients for services that are covered by TRICARE but not by Medicare. Thus, TFL provides Medicare-eligible military retirees age 65 or older with one of the most comprehensive health insurance benefit packages in the United States.

TFL was motivated by dissatisfaction among retiree groups with DoD-sponsored health benefits that were previously available to them. Prior to TFL, military retirees age 65 or over were entitled to care in military treatment facilities (MTFs) on a space-available basis but not to other DoD-sponsored health insurance benefits.[2] In particular, military retirees became ineligible for TRICARE coverage at age 65, when they became eligible for Medicare. Medicare benefits are generally less comprehensive and more expensive to the beneficiary than TRICARE benefits. Because military retirees believed that DoD had made a commitment to provide them with health insurance coverage for life,[3] groups representing retirees asked Congress to honor this "commitment" and enhance benefits for retirees. TFL and the new pharmacy benefit program for Medicare-eligible military retirees that was also included in the FY2001 NDAA were intended to address these concerns.

TFL is designed as a supplement to Medicare, similar to other employer-sponsored or privately purchased Medicare supplemental or "Medigap" policies. However, because TFL is based on the existing TRICARE program, the TFL benefits were not specifically designed to fit together with the Medicare benefits (in contrast to standard "Medigap" plans). As a result, there are benefit and coverage inconsistencies that pose operational challenges and

---

[1] Public Law 106-398, 114 Stat 1654.

[2] This policy followed the terms of Public Law 89-614, *Military Medical Benefits Amendments of 1966,* which established the Civilian Health and Medical Program of the Uniformed Service (CHAMPUS) program and limited coverage to beneficiaries under age 65.

[3] This perceived commitment is commonly referred to as "The Promise" by beneficiary organizations and even within TRICARE Management Activity (TMA), the office within the Department of Defense with responsibility for overseeing the administration of health benefits to military dependents and retirees.

raise policy issues. In the case of long-term care, services are not a covered benefit under either Medicare or TRICARE except for limited services provided by skilled nursing facilities in conjunction with certifiable medical need following an inpatient hospital stay or that are provided by home health agencies.

Prior to TFL, the federal government's financial obligations for health care provided to Medicare-eligible DoD military retirees was determined by where the care was furnished: Medicare was solely responsible for civilian care (for Medicare-covered benefits after application of beneficiary cost-sharing requirements), and DoD assumed all costs for space-available care provided by MTFs to Medicare beneficiaries. In FY2000, DoD spent an estimated $1.4 billion on direct care for dual eligibles (TRICARE Management Activity, 2001b). Under TFL, DoD continues to have sole responsibility for direct care but now also has responsibility as secondary payer for civilian care. DoD will spend an estimated $3.9 billion in secondary payments for civilian care furnished to Medicare beneficiaries (TRICARE Management Activity, 2001b).

Focus of This Study

This report examines the new TFL program with the goal of identifying areas that may pose policy and/or implementation issues. Where appropriate, the report suggests policy options that DoD could consider to

- make benefits more efficient, from the perspective of DoD, taxpayers, and beneficiaries (by considering changes in the benefit structure)
- promote easier operation of the TFL program (by improving benefit compatibility, for example)
- improve the overall benefit package for Medicare-eligible military beneficiaries.

Given the limited time and resources for this study, we focused on three types of issue areas: those that DoD specifically asked us to examine (such as managed care options, including the new TRICARE Plus program, and Medicare payments for MTF care); areas in which the Medicare and TRICARE benefits differ significantly (e.g., behavioral health care and coverage for certain emerging technologies); and areas of potential operational concern (e.g., medical necessity determinations).

Some of the issues identified here have already been addressed by Congress or the TRICARE Management Activity (TMA). Such cases are noted in this report.

Research Methodology

In conducting this research, we relied on several sources of information. We began with a comprehensive review of relevant policy manuals, literature, and other materials on both the Medicare and TRICARE programs to document and compare the eligibility requirements, benefit definitions, and coverage policies within each program. To inform our analysis, we also obtained quantitative data regarding the number and geographic distribution of Medicare-eligible military retirees from the TMA Health Program Analysis and Evaluation.[4] As appropriate, RAND Corporation staff received copies of internal DoD communications and briefing slides to inform the work. We also conducted a number of formal and informal interviews and discussions with

- key Department of Defense officials, including legal counsel, policymakers, and health program managers as well as appropriate TRICARE Management Activity operations staff responsible for TFL implementation
- representatives from each of the DoD Surgeons General offices (Army, Navy, and Air Force)
- representatives from beneficiary advocacy groups, such as the Retired Officers Association and the National Military Family Association, Inc.
- non-DoD experts knowledgeable in relevant health benefit areas, such as long-term care or emerging technologies.

In general, the interviews served several purposes, including

- refining the research questions and topic areas for the report
- clarifying TRICARE benefit policies with regard to coverage areas, special programs (e.g., TRICARE Plus), and claims processing
- documenting topics related to TFL implementation, such as implementation plans, goals for TRICARE Plus, and issues with TMA's communication with beneficiaries about TFL program benefits.

This work was also significantly informed by our review of relevant non-DoD health care literature written by various authors and the accumulated knowledge and experience of those authors in the specific areas they addressed.

The initial work for this report was conducted prior to TFL implementation on October 1, 2001. Since the TFL implementation, we have not updated the report to discuss experience under TFL or policy changes since TFL implementation (for example, subsequent changes in Medicare coverage policies). However, in Chapter Two, we did update our discussions of benefit coordination issues that have been addressed by subsequent legislation:

- The FY2002 National Defense Authorization Act (Public Law 107-107, December 28, 2001) addressed inconsistencies between Medicare and TRICARE regarding eligibility, coverage, and payment for post-acute care services (i.e., services provided by skilled nursing facilities and home health agencies).
- The FY2003 National Defense Authorization Act (Public Law 107-314) eliminated the prior authorization requirement for inpatient psychiatric services covered under Medicare. In addition, Section 705 of the FY2003 NDAA provides that a physician or other practitioner who is eligible to receive reimbursement for services under Medicare is also approved to provide care under TFL.

---

[4] See Military Health System, "Health Budgets and Financial Policy" website (http://www.ha.osd.mil/HBFP/default.cfm).

Organization of This Report

Chapter Two provides a basic summary of Medicare and TRICARE eligibility and entitlement requirements, describes Medicare and TRICARE's respective benefit structures, and discusses how these benefits are coordinated to cover health care services provided to the TFL-eligible population. It then focuses on several benefit areas with potential benefit inconsistencies or non-covered services. Chapter Three considers the implications of alternative beneficiary cost-sharing policies for civilian care. Chapter Four examines the opportunity for managing direct care services provided by MTFs through TRICARE Plus. Chapter Five discusses potential models for the Medicare program to share in the costs of MTF care furnished to TFL beneficiaries. Each chapter also includes a discussion of policy options. Chapter Six presents a summary of findings and recommendations on the areas examined in this report.

CHAPTER TWO

Medicare and TRICARE Benefits and Coverage Policies

This chapter examines issues raised by differences in Medicare and TRICARE benefit design and coverage policies. We begin with an overview of eligibility, benefits, coverage, and medical necessity determinations, and the appeals process under both programs. We then highlight specific areas—emerging technologies, post-acute care services, and behavioral health care—where there are differences between TRICARE and Medicare benefits, discuss how these differences are handled under TFL, and consider TRICARE's liability for payment.

For purposes of our discussion, the following definitions apply:

- Coverage policy is a population-based determination that a service is eligible for Medicare payment or TRICARE cost-sharing under certain conditions.
- Medical necessity determinations are made on specific claims based on whether the beneficiary meets the clinical criteria that have been established for coverage of the service.
- Payment determinations relate to the amount of Medicare payment that will be made for a medically necessary covered service.

Overview of Medicare and TRICARE Programs

Medicare has traditionally been administered as two separate entitlements: Hospital Insurance (Part A) and Supplemental Medical Insurance (Part B).[1] Part A coverage is generally provided automatically, free of premiums, to eligible persons. Most U.S. citizens age 65 or over are eligible for Medicare. In addition, Medicare covers the disabled and persons with end-stage renal disease. Coverage under Part B is based on voluntary enrollment and payment of a monthly premium ($58.70 in 2003). Beneficiaries who do not enroll in Part B at age 65 may do so later; however, in general, the Part B premium increases 10 percent for each year after age 65 that the beneficiary is not enrolled.

The TRICARE program was established in 1992 to create a comprehensive managed health care program for the delivery and financing of health care services in the Military

---

[1] The statutory provisions for Medicare are in Title 18 of the Social Security Act, designated "Health Insurance for the Aged and Disabled." Entitlement for Medicare is specified in 42 Code of Federal Regulations (CFR) 406. The Balanced Budget Act of 1997 also introduced a third part, sometimes known as Part C, the Medicare+Choice program, which expanded beneficiaries' options for participation in private-sector health care plans.

Health System (MHS).[2] TRICARE generally covers all active duty personnel and military retirees and their eligible dependents. To be eligible for TRICARE for Life, a person must be a military retiree, survivor, or dependent who is entitled to Medicare Part A, 65 years of age or older, and enrolled in Medicare Part B.[3]

For military beneficiaries under age 65, the TRICARE program offers benefit options, known as TRICARE Prime, Standard, and Extra. TRICARE Prime is essentially a health maintenance organization; the provider network consists primarily of military treatment facilities (the "direct care" system), supplemented by authorized care from designated civilian providers (the "purchased care" system). Beneficiaries who enroll in TRICARE Prime receive priority access to care at MTFs, are generally locked into the designated provider network, and are required to follow the referral and utilization management guidance of a primary care manager. Worldwide, the services operated 76 hospitals and 460 clinics in 2001 (Department of Defense, 2002). TRICARE Standard and Extra collectively function essentially as a preferred provider organization. TRICARE Extra covers the use of in-network providers, and Standard covers the use of out-of-network providers. Beneficiaries who do not enroll in TRICARE Prime are automatically eligible for TRICARE Standard/Extra; these beneficiaries remain eligible for MTF care on a space-available basis, with low priority.

Before TFL, military retirees became ineligible for TRICARE at age 65, although they remained eligible for MTF care on a space-available basis with the same low priority as other retirees who are not enrolled in TRICARE Prime. TFL requires no enrollment (beyond enrollment in Medicare Part B) and no premiums. In general, TFL beneficiaries remain eligible for MTF care on a space-available basis. However, as discussed in greater detail in Chapter Four, some beneficiaries are being offered priority access to MTF primary care under a new program called TRICARE Plus, which was developed concurrently with TFL.

Comparison of Medicare and TRICARE Benefits

Most health care services that are covered benefits under TRICARE are also covered benefits under Medicare, and vice versa. In general, TFL covers Medicare's cost-sharing requirements for services that are covered by both programs. TFL does not cover Medicare's cost-sharing unless the service is also covered by TRICARE. If a service is covered by TRICARE but not by Medicare, TFL beneficiaries face the same access and cost-sharing rules as other TRICARE beneficiaries.[4]

Table 2.1 is a side-by-side comparison of benefits that are eligible for payment under Medicare and TRICARE. In general, these benefits are largely comparable. However, there are several areas of inconsistency in either benefits covered, coverage limits, and/or

---

[2] Entitlement to TRICARE benefits is defined in Title 10 of the U.S. Code. With a few exceptions, those eligible for TRICARE must be listed in the Defense Enrollment Eligibility Reporting System (DEERS) in order to receive care.

[3] More specifically, only the following persons are eligible: a retired uniformed service member or a dependent (except for parents and parents-in-law) of a retired uniformed service member; a member who died while on active duty for more than 30 days; or a member who died from an injury, illness or disease incurred or aggravated while on active duty for less than 31 days, was in training, or was traveling to or from a place of duty; or an un-remarried former eligible spouse who does not have an employer-sponsored health plan (see 10 U.S.C. 1071(2)).

[4] TRICARE beneficiaries have a $3,000 per year catastrophic cap, beyond which TRICARE provides 100 percent coverage.

Table 2.1
Summary of Medicare Benefits Versus TRICARE Benefits—Medicare Part A

Benefit	Medicare 2003 Benefits	TRICARE Benefits	Areas of Concern for TFL
Inpatient hospitalization, Medical-surgical benefits (per benefit period)[a]	Day 1–60: no member cost-sharing after $840 deductible Day 61–90: member copayment of $210 per day Day 90–150: member copayment of $420 per day Day 151 and up: not covered, but 60 lifetime reserve days are available	Unlimited coverage for authorized inpatient care	
Inpatient hospitalization, psychiatric	Limited to 190 days in a psychiatric hospital; rules same as medical-surgical if in a general hospital	Preauthorization required; limited to 30 days per fiscal year	TRICARE preauthorization requirements; statutory limitations on covered days
Inpatient hospitalization, emergency	Covered inside and outside United States and in non-participating hospitals	Covered inside and outside of United States and in non-participating hospitals	
Skilled nursing facilities (SNFs) per benefit period	Eligibility: Admission must be preceded by a qualifying three-day hospital stay, and patient must require skilled nursing or rehab at least five times per week Coverage and copayments: Day 1–20: 100% covered Day 21–100: all but $105 covered Day 101 and up: not covered	Eligibility: FY2002 NDAA established same criteria as Medicare Coverage and copayments: No day limits; 25% coinsurance applies after 100 days when TRICARE becomes primary payer	Differences in prequalifying criteria were resolved by TRICARE adopting Medicare's criteria No limits on skilled nursing facility care Potential for some Medicare-covered services after 100 days
Home health benefits	Eligibility: Patient must be homebound and require part-time intermittent skilled nursing care or therapy[b] Coverage: 100% for intermittent part-time skilled nursing and home health aide services, therapy services, and medical social services	TRICARE benefits conform to Medicare definitions in the FY2002 authorization	No benefits for patients who need more than intermittent part-time nursing care
Hospice	Available only to individuals who are terminally ill. Covers two 90-day periods, a subsequent 30-day period, plus a subsequent extension period if required. Provides full cost, except for copayments for drugs and respite for inpatient care. Includes continuous home care during a period of crisis and nursing and doctors' services.	No current limits; covers physician care, nursing, medical social services, short-term inpatient care (both general and respite, but respite limited to no more than five consecutive days at a time). Includes medical supplies, durable medical equipment (DME).	Whether Medicare hospice election is deemed a TRICARE hospice enrollment

[a] A benefit period begins with an initial hospitalization and ends when the beneficiary has not received hospital or skilled nursing care for 60 days in a row.

[b] Also covered under Part B; similar eligibility and benefit definitions apply.

Table 2.2
Summary of Medicare Benefits Versus TRICARE Benefits—Medicare Part B

Benefit	Medicare Benefits	TRICARE Benefits	Areas of Concern for TFL
Physician visits	Covers 80% of approved charges after yearly deductible	Payment based on CHAMPUS Maximum Allowable Charge (CMAC), usually 75% or 80% of allowable charges depending on beneficiary's copayment/coinsurance rate	
Podiatry	Excludes routine foot care; medical foot care for vascular disease; metabolic or neurologic disease may be covered	Similar to Medicare	
Ophthalmology and optometry	Medically necessary vision care if provided by optometrist or ophthalmologist (if in connection with medical or surgical treatment of covered illness); routine vision care and eye glasses are excluded	Similar to Medicare	
Dental	Covered if medically necessary and done as integral part of a covered procedure	Similar to Medicare; routine dental care excluded for all non-active-duty beneficiaries (and family)	
Chiropractic	Covers manual manipulation of spine to correct subluxation	Excluded	
Nursing		Covered; usually 80% of allowable charges	TRICARE does not require physician visit every 30 days.
Occupational and physical therapy	Covered if prescribed by physician and reviewed every 30 days	Services that are aimed at reducing severity of impaired function are covered	Medicare does not cover services provided by speech language pathologists or audiologists (other than diagnostic tests) in independent practice
Speech and audiology services	Covered if prescribed by physician and reviewed every 30 days	Services can be covered if medically necessary	
Emergency room visit	Covers 80%	Covers 80%	
Radiology and other diagnostic tests	Covers diagnostic X-rays and 100% of approved laboratory services	Covers approved and necessary laboratory and diagnostic X-rays	
Durable medical equipment and supplies	Covered under Part A for use in hospital; covered under Part B at 80%	Covered for outpatient use if ordered by a physician, $100 minimum	Coinsurance for items costing less than $100
Outpatient hospital services	Covered; coinsurance or copayment varies according to service	Covered	
Mental health visits	Covers 50% of allowable charges for outpatient visits to qualified providers	Covers up to 80% of allowable charges for outpatient visits to qualified providers; preauthorization requirements for more than eight psychotherapy visits	Definition of and limits on benefit periods; preauthorization requirements for psychotherapy visits beyond eight visits
Drugs and biologics	Covers costs of non-self-administered drugs and biologics and oral cancer drugs	Covers outpatient formulary medications, copayments vary depending on where the prescription is filled and whether the drug is brand name or generic	

preauthorization requirements. For example, certain chiropractic services are covered by Medicare but not by TRICARE, and services provided by Christian Science practitioners are covered by TRICARE but not by Medicare. In addition, Medicare and TRICARE have differing policies with regard to benefit limits and preauthorization for services in some areas, such as mental health and skilled nursing facility services.

Comparison of Coverage and Medical Necessity Determinations

The Medicare law does not list the specific items and services eligible for coverage under the Medicare program. Rather, it vests the Secretary of the Department of Health and Human Services (DHHS) with authority to make decisions about which specific items and services within the broad benefit categories can be covered by Medicare under a general requirement that no payment is to be made for services that are not "reasonable" and "necessary" for the diagnosis and treatment of an illness or injury.[5] The individual contractors that process claims for Medicare make most coverage decisions. Issues that involve significant scientific or medical controversy, that potentially have a major impact on the Medicare program, or that are subject to broad public controversy may be raised to the national level and become national coverage policy. National coverage determinations are binding on all Medicare contractors.[6]

In contrast, TRICARE benefits and coverage policies are set by legislation, guided by Title 10 of the U.S. Code, and outlined in a comprehensive set of TRICARE policy manuals and implemented by five TRICARE Managed Care Support Contractors[7] (MCSC) covering 12 geographical health care regions within the United States. The *Managed Care Support Contract Operations Manual* guides each MCSC in implementing these policies. In addition, TRICARE's Quality and Utilization Review Peer Review Organization Program assists in monitoring utilization, reviewing claims, and considering appeals for coverage. Currently, private contractors process TRICARE claims.

Both Medicare and TRICARE require that services or supplies be medically necessary in order to be covered. While the wording of their medical necessity statements varies slightly,[8] the basic intent remains the same: that the service or supply is reasonable and necessary for the diagnosis or treatment of an illness or injury. The TRICARE definition is more expansive than Medicare's; in particular, it includes preventive services and services intended to sustain a patient's current condition. TRICARE also provides benefits to beneficiaries of all ages, including children. When a service or item is a benefit of both TRICARE and

---

[5] Coverage policies are defined in the Social Security Act (e.g., Sections 1812 and 1861), in the Code of Federal Regulations (42 CFR), and in several manuals produced by the Center for Medicare and Medicaid Services.

[6] The process by which Medicare makes a national coverage decision is outlined in the *Federal Register,* April 27, 1999 (64 FR 22619–22625).

[7] These contracts were to be renegotiated in FY2003.

[8] The medical necessity definitions are as follows:
Medicare: Items and services must be considered reasonable and necessary for the diagnosis and treatment of illness or injury or to improve the functioning of a malformed body member to be eligible for payment.
TRICARE: The frequency, extent, and types of medical services or supplies must represent appropriate medical care and be generally accepted by qualified professionals to be reasonable and adequate for the diagnosis and treatment of illness, injury, pregnancy, and mental disorders or that are reasonable and adequate for well-baby care.

Medicare, TFL relies on Medicare's medical necessity review and determination. That is, if a dually covered service claim is denied for reimbursement from Medicare on the basis of medical necessity, TRICARE will not consider the claim for TFL cost-sharing. In cases in which a Medicare claim is denied because it is for a service that is not covered by Medicare, TRICARE will accept the claim for processing and determine whether the item or service is eligible for cost-sharing or payment under current TRICARE policies.

DoD regulations implementing the TFL program concentrate on differences in basic categories of benefits, such as Medicare's coverage of certain chiropractic services or TRICARE's outpatient drug benefit, and how claims for those services will be handled. The regulations do not specifically deal with differences where the basic benefit category is the same; for example, both programs cover inpatient hospital services, but the specific service in question (e.g., pancreas transplant) is not covered by one of the two programs because it is not "reasonable and necessary" in accordance with standard medical practice.

A potential concern for TFL is whether the coding specificity in Medicare's claims determination is sufficient for TRICARE to distinguish between Medicare coverage and medical necessity determinations and establish its cost-sharing liability accurately. For example, the Medicare contractor may make a medical necessity denial on a claim for a procedure that is not covered for the patient's condition but is covered for other conditions; e.g., Medicare covers positron emission tomography (PET) scans for only certain indications. If TRICARE typically covers the procedure for the patient's condition, a concern could be raised that Medicare's denial based on medical necessity might preclude TRICARE from reviewing and considering the claim for payment. TMA has indicated that the claim denial codes used by the Medicare contractors should be sufficient for TRICARE's purposes, but this hinges on an empirical question that will need to be evaluated in practice.

Comparison of Denials and Appeals

Both Medicare and TRICARE beneficiaries have appeal rights when a claim for health care services or supplies has been denied. For TFL beneficiaries, TMA has indicated that the Medicare appeals process takes precedence for services that are covered by both Medicare and TRICARE. DoD regulations provide that "services and supplies denied payment by Medicare would not be considered for coverage by TRICARE if the Medicare denial is appealable under the Medicare appeals process."[9] The policy should be reviewed to ensure that it is working as intended for Medicare denials involving national coverage determinations that cover a service for specified conditions only. If the patient's condition does not meet the established criteria, the denial may be appealed. However, the appeal is essentially pro forma because the coverage policy is binding on the hearing office or administrative law judge. Because the decision may be appealed under Medicare, it is possible that TRICARE will not consider the claim for coverage even though the service is a TRICARE covered benefit, would meet TRICARE conditions for medical necessity, and would be covered for the TRICARE non-Medicare population.

---

[9] 32 CFR 199.10.

Comparison of Coverage for Emerging Technologies

Emerging technology is one area that may require special attention from DoD. Almost by definition, coverage policies for emerging technologies are continuously evolving in both TRICARE and Medicare, as new technology is disseminated and additional information becomes available on the safety and efficacy of specific technologies. Medicare's coverage policies for a particular technology at a particular point in time may conflict with those that TRICARE has established for beneficiaries under age 65. In addition, Medicare policies may vary geographically by contractor.

Medicare's process for making coverage policy has become increasingly evidence based and public, and Medicare's coverage of emerging technologies has expanded. One result of Medicare's expanding coverage is that TRICARE's coverage policies currently appear to be more restrictive than Medicare's in areas in which both programs have specified the indications or conditions for which a certain technology will be covered. In addition, the Medicare program has issued policies on a broader range of procedures.

Policies pertaining to coverage of devices and drugs that are regulated by the Food and Drug Administration (FDA) are fairly similar. Under both programs, an FDA determination that the regulated drug or device is "safe and effective" is necessary but not sufficient for coverage. Medicare requires clinical data supporting a determination that the technology is "reasonable and necessary" for diagnosis and treatment of the Medicare population. Similarly, TRICARE requires reliable evidence that the technology is medically necessary and in accordance with nationally accepted standards of practice in the medical community.

TRICARE and Medicare also have similar policies with regard to investigational devices undergoing the FDA's pre-market approval process for devices that represent a potentially significant risk of illness or injury. TRICARE and Medicare's policies for off-label uses of drugs and devices are also similar.

Potential Differences in Coverage Policies for New Technologies

Although the general policies are the same, coverage determinations for specific technologies are frequently complex and involve both medical necessity determinations and payment determinations as well as application of specific coverage policies. We assume that TRICARE will follow Medicare's coverage policies when it has not established its own coverage policy for a new technology. However, as discussed above, it is not clear how different coverage policies that are based on whether a service is reasonable and necessary in accordance with standard medical practice without regard to an individual patient's medical condition will be handled. We can envision the following situations:

- If Medicare covers a certain technology and TRICARE does not, a decision to follow Medicare's determination that the service is medically necessary would result in the service being treated differently for the under-65 TRICARE population than the TFL population. Not covering the service will raise the issue of why TRICARE does not consider the service to be medically necessary when Medicare does.
- If Medicare does not cover a technology and TRICARE does, a decision to follow Medicare's determination means that the TFL beneficiary would not receive the same benefits that are extended to the rest of the TRICARE population. Paying for the

service would raise the issue of why Medicare does not consider the service to be medically necessary when TRICARE does.

Opportunities for different coverage policies for emerging technologies could arise under the three situations described next.

Scenario 1: Medicare Has a National Coverage Policy. The Center for Medicare and Medicaid Services (CMS) considers making national coverage policy determinations for emerging technologies when there are inconsistencies in local coverage policy determinations, substantial disagreement among medical experts regarding whether the technology is reasonable and necessary, and/or when there is potential for over-utilization of the technology with significant impact on program expenditures. When there are national Medicare coverage policies, Medicare benefits are uniform for all beneficiaries, regardless of place of residence. While denials may be appealed, the coverage policy is binding on the hearing officer or administrative law judge.

Scenario 2: Medicare Has No National Coverage Policy. Under Medicare, most coverage policies on emerging technology are made at the local contractor level in part because there is inadequate or no scientific evidence available to establish a national coverage policy. The general questions that a contractor asks in developing local medical review policy are: Is the product safe and effective? Is it reasonable and necessary? Is it experimental or investigational? In determining the answer to these questions, contractors draw on existing coverage policies and guidance and seek input from local medical advisory committees. Leaving the determinations to be made at the local level allows for some technology diffusion but also creates the potential for coverage of a new technology in one geographic area but not in another. Thus, as is the case with other Medicare beneficiaries, Medicare may cover a technology for some TFL beneficiaries but not for others.

Scenario 3: Medicare-Covered Clinical Trials. The Medicare program pays for routine patient care costs and costs due to medical complications associated with participation in qualifying clinical trials. A qualifying trial evaluates a service that (1) falls within a Medicare benefit category; (2) has a therapeutic intent (e.g., is not designed solely to test toxicity); (3) enrolls diagnosed beneficiaries rather than healthy volunteers; and (4) is funded by a federal agency or a cooperative center funded by a federal agency, or is a drug trial that is exempt from having an Investigational New Drug application. CMS maintains a Medicare clinical trials registry for qualifying trials. The following applies to qualifying trials:

- Routine costs are covered for Medicare beneficiaries in both the experimental group and the control group. Routine costs include medically necessary conventional care that would be provided absent a clinical trial, services required for the provision of the investigational item or service (e.g., administration of a non-covered cancer drug), and services required for monitoring or diagnosis and treatment of complications.

- The investigational device itself is not covered under the national coverage determination for clinical trials. In addition, items and services provided as part of the clinical trial are not covered if they are (1) needed solely for data collection and analysis, (2) customarily provided by the research sponsors free of charge, or (3) provided solely to determine trial eligibility (Health Care Financing Administration, 2001a and 2001b).

As a general policy, TRICARE does not cover clinical trials; however, DoD has a demonstration project to cover National Cancer Institute–sponsored Phase II and Phase III cancer treatment and prevention clinical trials. Unlike Medicare, TRICARE will cover screening costs to determine eligibility to participate in the cancer clinical trial in addition to the medical costs associated with participation (other than the investigational drugs). Also, Medicare does not generally cover cancer-prevention trials because the program's coverage of preventive services is also limited.

Comparison of Coverage Policies for Selected Technologies

In Table 2.3, we summarize the differences between Medicare and TRICARE policies regarding covered services. We do not list those technologies for which the policies appear to be consistent. Further, the summary is not intended to be an all-inclusive list. Rather, it is intended to highlight the sorts of questions that may arise due to the differences between the two programs. Those issues include the following:

1. Does TRICARE's reliance on Medicare medical necessity determinations extend to services for which TRICARE has established a more restrictive coverage policy? For example, will TRICARE assume secondary-payer liability for a Medicare-covered PET scan for colorectal cancer or for a Medicare-covered pancreas transplant following a kidney transplant? (These services are currently excluded from TRICARE coverage as not being proven to be safe and effective, but they are covered under the Medicare program.) If TRICARE does not assume secondary-payer liability, what payment policies will apply to hospital and physician services that are furnished in conjunction with the non-covered services?

2. If TRICARE ordinarily covers a service that Medicare does not cover to treat a specific condition, will TRICARE treat Medicare's denial as a medical necessity denial or as a non-covered service? For example, will TRICARE assume primary-payer liability for a PET scan performed for an indication[10] that is not covered by Medicare, e.g., a PET scan for the diagnosis and management of seizure disorders?

3. Will TRICARE cover as the primary-payer certain services that are furnished by a non-Medicare covered provider? For example, a broader range of providers of biofeedback therapy is covered under TRICARE than under Medicare. Will TRICARE cover biofeedback therapy as the primary payer when a TRICARE-authorized non-physician provider furnishes the service?

We believe that TFL will highlight coverage inconsistencies between TRICARE and Medicare and may create pressure for consistent "federal" coverage policy. As a general rule, there should be a clear rationale for why a specific technology is covered by one program and not the other. Because the two programs cover different populations, there may be some technologies for which the same level of coverage under both programs is not appropriate. However, both programs apply a "reasonable and necessary" standard that takes into account

---

[10] A sign or a circumstance that points to or shows the cause, pathology, treatment, or outcome of an attack of disease.

Table 2.3
Differences Between Medicare and TRICARE Covered Services

Procedure	Medicare Coverage Policy	TRICARE Coverage Policy
Allogeneic bone marrow transplantation	Medicare covers at least three indications that are explicitly excluded from TRICARE coverage: 1. Advanced Hodgkin's disease, in cases in which conventional therapy has failed and there is no human leukocyte antigen (HLA)-matched donor 2. Neuroblastoma 3. Multiple myeloma, in cases in which the beneficiary has newly diagnosed Durie-Salmon Stage II or III or responsive multiple myeloma with adequate cardiac, renal, pulmonary and hepatic functioning.	More restrictive; see Medicare description.
Ambulatory blood pressure monitoring	Medicare has not made a national coverage policy determination. Local carrier coverage determinations are being made (although CMS has a national coverage determination pending).	TRICARE has determined that it is a non-covered procedure of unproven value.
Biofeedback as an initial treatment modality for urinary incontinence	Medicare has a national coverage policy determination that covers biofeedback for patients with stress and/or urge incontinence who have already undergone and failed a trial of pelvic muscle exercises. CMS leaves it to the discretion of the contractor whether to approve coverage for the use of biofeedback as an initial treatment modality for urinary incontinence. Medicare requires that biofeedback be provided by a physician or "incident-to" a physician's service, i.e., under the direct supervision of the physician.	TRICARE covers adjunctive treatment for muscle re-education of specific muscle groups when the patient's condition is not responding to other forms of conventional treatment (which appears to preclude coverage for biofeedback as an initial treatment modality). TRICARE requires that biofeedback therapy be provided by a TRICARE-authorized provider (i.e., either a physician or provider to whom the patient has been referred).
Pancreas transplantation	Medicare covers a pancreas transplant when it is performed simultaneously or after a kidney transplant for beneficiaries with end-stage chronic renal disease (ESRD) and Type I or Type II Diabetes Mellitus.	TRICARE covers simultaneous kidney-pancreas transplantation for beneficiaries who have concomitant ESRD and Type I Diabetes Mellitus that are resistant to exogenous therapy. Pancreas transplants alone, including after kidney transplantation, are not covered.
Percutaneous transluminal angioplasty (PTA) of the carotid artery	Medicare will cover PTA of the carotid artery when it is furnished to an inpatient concurrent with a carotid stent replacement under an approved Category B clinical trial.	TRICARE's policy manual contains a general exclusion for PTA of the carotid artery and makes no mention of when it is performed concurrent with a carotid stent replacement.
Positron emission tomography	Medicare covers PET scans for imaging of the perfusion of the heart; characterization of solitary pulmonary nodules and initial staging of lung disease; and evaluation of recurrent colorectal cancer, staging lymphoma, or staging recurrent melanoma prior to surgery. CMS is currently evaluating for national coverage determinations for Alzheimer's disease, breast cancer, myocardial viability, and thyroid cancer.	TRICARE's covered indications are diagnosis and management of seizure disorders, evaluation of ischemic heart disease, and diagnosis and management of lung cancer. In addition, the TRICARE policy manual states that PET scans for other indications are covered when reliable evidence supports that the use of a PET scan is safe, effective, and comparable or superior to standard care (i.e., proven). However, TRICARE explicitly excludes PET scans for a number of indications, including colorectal cancer (one of the Medicare-covered indications).

medical evidence and standard medical practice and should result in similar coverage determinations. TMA is not represented on the CMS Medicare Coverage Advisory Committee (MCAC). Coordination between the two programs could be enhanced if TMA became an active participant in the MCAC deliberations (as it was on the predecessor Medicare Technology Assessment Committee). TMA's participation in the committee would give TMA the opportunity to have input into the coverage determination process and to make deliberate judgments regarding whether TRICARE's coverage policies should deviate from Medicare's.

Comparison of Post-Acute Care Benefits

The term "post-acute care" is generally applied to rehabilitation and long-term hospital inpatient stays, skilled nursing facility care, home health agency (HHA) services, and outpatient therapy services. The term is somewhat of a misnomer in that HHA services and outpatient therapy services are not limited to care following an acute illness episode and can involve medical needs for chronic conditions. In this subsection, we focus on coordination of benefit issues involving skilled nursing facility (SNF), HHA, and outpatient rehabilitation services furnished to meet either post-acute or chronic care needs. We have not identified any issues specific to inpatient rehabilitation hospital stays.

Coverage for Skilled Nursing Facility Services

Medicare coverage for skilled nursing facility care is contingent on a three-day qualifying hospital stay ending within seven days of the SNF admission (or 14 days under certain circumstances). A patient is defined as needing an SNF level of care if skilled care or skilled rehabilitative care is furnished on a daily basis (five times per week for therapy) that as a practical matter can only be provided on an inpatient basis. Custodial care is not covered under the Medicare program.[11]

Prior to TFL (and the expansion of benefits to those age 65 or over), TRICARE beneficiaries had very little need for SNF services. As a result, few restrictions were placed on the SNF benefits. No qualifying hospital stay was required, no limits were set on the duration of medically necessary SNF services, and SNF providers were paid for the billed charges. The FY2002 National Defense Authorization Act (Public Law 107-107) addressed inconsistencies between Medicare and TRICARE regarding eligibility for SNF care and the payment rates that apply when TRICARE is the primary payer. With these changes, eligibility for SNF coverage parallels Medicare's requirement for a three-day qualifying hospital stay. TRICARE is liable for the beneficiary's coinsurance amounts for days 20 through 100 of an SNF stay. However, no limitations are placed on the duration of the TRICARE SNF benefit. Beginning with day 101, when Medicare SNF benefits are exhausted, TRICARE covers 75 percent of allowed charges, and the TFL beneficiary is responsible for the remaining 25 percent. TRICARE has adopted the Medicare prospective payment per diem rates and applies Medicare's level of care criteria in making medical necessity determinations (Department of Defense, 2002).

---

[11] Medicare defines *custodial care* as follows: Treatment of services regardless of who recommends them or where they are provided, that could be rendered safely and easily by a person not medically skilled, or that are designed mainly to help the patient with activities of daily living.

Two areas of potential concern remain for DoD regarding how TFL is being implemented with respect to SNF care. The first is the lack of any limitation on the duration of SNF benefits. For the first 100 days, TFL beneficiaries have no cost-sharing liabilities and, as a result, no financial incentives to seek care from less-costly alternatives. After 100 days, when there is 25 percent cost-sharing with TRICARE, TFL beneficiaries have some incentive to find alternative care settings. However, with home health care limited to part-time and intermittent care, some beneficiaries with skilled nursing needs may find that continuing SNF care is an attractive option. We discuss this issue further in the subsection below on home health benefits.

A second area of potential concern involves services after day 101. Medicare's per diem prospective payment rates are all-inclusive rates that cover all medically necessary services provided by the SNF. For covered Part A stays, Medicare's consolidated billing provision requires the SNF to bill directly for all services (regardless of whether they are provided by the SNF or by an outside supplier under arrangements with the SNF) that are not expressly excluded from the provision.[12] When Medicare SNF benefits are exhausted, certain medical and other health services (e.g., diagnostic tests and therapy services) furnished to an SNF resident are covered under Part B of the Medicare program. These are services that would have been covered by the Medicare per diem payment for a covered Part A stay.

TRICARE adopted Medicare's per diem prospective payment system and consolidated billing requirements, effective August 1, 2003 (TRICARE Management Activity, 2002a, p. 27). The new provider agreement requires the SNF to accept TRICARE payment as the full payment and to not bill TRICARE beneficiaries for other than applicable cost-sharing amounts. TRICARE's all-inclusive per diem payment to the facility using the Medicare payment rates includes services that would be covered under Part B of the Medicare program. Presumably, the SNF would not bill Medicare for these services under the terms of its provider agreement with TRICARE. In theory, however, Medicare should continue as primary payer for the Part B services, and TRICARE's payment should be net of any Medicare Part B payments.

Potential TFL savings could be generated by requiring that the SNF bill for any Part B services furnished to patients in a TRICARE-covered inpatient stay and making TRICARE's per diem payment to the SNF net of any Medicare payments made for those services. However, the administrative costs associated with applying this policy need to be considered. Unless a substantial number of TFL beneficiaries remain in the SNF after 100 days, the potential savings that would be generated by offsetting Medicare's payments may not be significant enough to warrant the added administrative burden. The effect on beneficiary cost-sharing would also need to be considered before implementing the policy.

Coverage for Home Health Care

To be eligible for home health care from a Medicare participating HHA, a beneficiary must be homebound, under a plan of care established by a physician, and need one or more of the following:

---

[12] The excluded services include the professional component of physician services (but not the technical component) and other professional services covered under Part B, certain hospital outpatient and dialysis-related services, ambulance services, and hospice care related to the beneficiary's terminal condition.

- intermittent skilled nursing care
- physical therapy
- speech-language pathology
- a continuous need for occupational therapy after one of the other qualifying services is no longer needed.

For eligibility purposes, intermittent skilled nursing care is defined as care that is needed or provided on fewer than seven days per week or less than eight hours per day for periods of 21 days or less. Extensions during the 21-day period are permitted when the need for additional care is finite and predictable.

Medicare beneficiaries who are eligible for home health care may receive

- part-time or intermittent skilled nursing and home health aide services
- physical therapy, speech language pathology, and occupational therapy
- medical social services
- medical supplies, durable medical equipment (DME), and injectible osteoporosis drugs.

For coverage purposes, the skilled nursing and home health aide services may be furnished on any number of days provided that in combination they are furnished less than eight hours per day and 28 or fewer hours per week (or, subject to case review, 35 or fewer hours per week). Medicare makes a prospective payment covering all services other than DME and injectible osteoporosis drugs provided during a 60-day episode. The payment is adjusted for clinical severity, functional severity, and service utilization. Medicare beneficiaries have no coinsurance liabilities for HHA services other than 20 percent coinsurance on DME and injectible osteoporosis drugs.

The TRICARE benefit for HHA services differed considerably from the Medicare benefit prior to the FY2002 NDAA: Eligibility was not contingent on being homebound or needing services on an intermittent part-time basis. The FY2002 NDAA changed TRICARE HHA benefits so that they conform to Medicare's coverage policies. With these changes, TRICARE should have no liability for HHA services provided to a TFL beneficiary because all medically necessary services would be covered by Medicare's prospective payment system. These changes also mean, however, that a beneficiary who needs more than intermittent, part-time care receives no added HHA benefit under the TFL program.

Policy Option: Expand HHA Coverage

In order to be eligible for home health services under Medicare, a beneficiary must need one of the four qualifying services listed above. A beneficiary who needs skilled nursing care on more than an intermittent part-time basis may still qualify for home health services as long as there is a need for one of the other qualifying services. In this situation, Medicare would cover intermittent part-time skilled nursing and home health aide services as well as other medically necessary home health services, and the beneficiary would be liable for paying for skilled nursing services in excess of 28 hours per week.

As currently structured, TRICARE would not cover the additional skilled services because the home health benefit is limited to "intermittent" skilled nursing services that are already being covered by Medicare. One option would be for TRICARE to cover the additional services. In essence, this would involve a legislative change that would make the *need* for skilled nursing care (without the "intermittent" requirement) one of the qualifying services for TRICARE-covered home health services. It would continue to limit TRICARE *coverage* to intermittent part-time skilled nursing and home health aide services so that in total the TFL beneficiary could be covered for up to 56 hours of skilled nursing care. The change could apply to both TFL beneficiaries and beneficiaries under age 65 (who would be responsible for paying for the additional care but would no longer be precluded from receiving any home health benefits if they needed more than intermittent skilled nursing care).

A question that would need to be addressed is, what would be an appropriate TRICARE payment in these situations? Medicare would remain the primary payer for up to 28 hours of the skilled nursing and home health aide services and the therapy and medical social services. One option would be for TRICARE to pay for the additional skilled nursing and home health services on a per-visit basis up to the amount that TRICARE would pay as primary payer. The per-visit rate could be based on Medicare's wage-adjusted rates by discipline that apply to low-utilization episodes (those with fewer than five visits).

TRICARE's liabilities and beneficiary utilization could be controlled by imposing coinsurance and capping TRICARE payments at 75 percent of a 60-day episode payment. The beneficiary would be liable for any remaining services. This approach would shift liability from the Medicare program to TRICARE for beneficiaries who would otherwise be receiving Medicare-covered SNF care to meet their daily skilled nursing needs. However, as discussed in the next section, it would be in TRICARE's financial interest to facilitate discharges of long-stay SNF cases.

Those home health patients who initially need more than intermittent skilled nursing care but qualify for Medicare home health aide services because they also need another qualifying home health service are likely to lose Medicare coverage after one or two 60-day episodes when the other qualifying service is no longer medically necessary. The loss of Medicare coverage could create pressure for TRICARE to become the primary payer for all medically necessary services, i.e., pay for more than intermittent part-time skilled nursing and home health aide services. Because these patients have benefited from combined Medicare/TRICARE coverage for up to 56 hours of skilled nursing care, limiting TRICARE benefits to part-time intermittent services at this point could be seen as a benefit reduction. It may be possible to control this perception if it is clear from the outset that TRICARE pays for only intermittent part-time skilled nursing and home health services but will supplement Medicare covered services when more than intermittent skilled nursing care is needed and any coverage reduction is in Medicare benefits rather than TRICARE benefits.

Policy Option: Cover Alternatives to SNF Care

The prior option would apply to all TFL beneficiaries. This option would confine the home care alternatives to beneficiaries who would otherwise qualify for continuing skilled nursing facility care, e.g., those who require daily skilled nursing care (or skilled rehabilitative care five times per week) following a three-day qualifying hospital stay.

There are alternative ways that financial assistance could be provided to this group of beneficiaries to enable them to receive services in a community-based setting. In each, TRICARE's liability would be limited to what its liability would be for SNF care (the coinsurance amount or 75 percent of the per diem rate) and would continue only so long as the beneficiary continued to need an SNF-level of care. For beneficiaries who are discharged from a Medicare-covered SNF stay and continue to need daily skilled nursing care, the option would pay for medically necessary home health services to the extent that they are not covered by the Medicare program. If the policy were to be budget neutral, TRICARE's payment would be based on (1) what would have been paid if the SNF stay had continued (and, including the SNF days, would be zero for up to the first 20 days, the SNF coinsurance amount for days 20 through 100, and 75 percent of the per diem thereafter) or (2) an actuarial estimate of the average TRICARE liability for SNF stays. However, beneficiary needs could be met more fully if a higher limit (e.g., 75 percent of the per diem rate) were applicable from the outset.

One alternative would be to confine coverage to services provided by Medicare-participating home health agencies. This option has the advantages of building in some quality assurance and the maximum opportunity for Medicare's sharing in the cost of caring for these patients in the community. In essence, it would extend to this subset of TFL beneficiaries the home health services that are provided for disabled dependents under the FY2002 NDAA. However, it does not provide the beneficiary with the flexibility to choose other sources of daily skilled nursing or rehabilitative care.

A "cash and counseling" option that pays the beneficiary a fixed monthly amount based on a percentage of the market cost of services is another alternative. This option would provide greater flexibility to tailor the purchase of community-based services to an individual beneficiary's needs.

Comparison of Coverage of Outpatient Rehabilitation Services

In this section, we discuss differences in the Medicare and TRICARE benefits for outpatient rehabilitation services provided to beneficiaries with post-acute and/or chronic care needs. The issues for these services primarily stem from differences in the settings and health care professionals who can furnish and bill for the services. Until these differences are resolved, this situation could lead to inconsistencies in payment and implementation difficulties. Some of these issues may be resolved by Section 705 of the FY2003 NDAA, which provides that a physician or practitioner who is eligible to receive reimbursement for services under Medicare is also approved to provide services under TFL.

Outpatient Rehabilitation Therapy
Medicare covers outpatient therapy services provided by the following:

- Hospital outpatient departments
- Therapists "incident to" physician services
- Comprehensive outpatient rehabilitation facilities (CORFs)
- Outpatient physical therapy providers and clinics (OPTs)
- Physical therapists and occupational therapists in independent practice
- Skilled nursing facility services for Medicare inpatients not receiving covered Part A SNF services.

All outpatient therapy sessions are paid under the physician fee schedule, including those furnished by hospital outpatient departments.[13] We have identified several areas as being potentially problematic. One area concerns how services furnished by CORFs and outpatient physical therapy providers will be handled by TRICARE as a secondary payer. These entities do not appear in the current listing of TRICARE authorized providers (in 32 CFR 199.6(f)). TRICARE regulations (32 CFR 199.6(f)) establish a special category for corporate services providers to accommodate individual professional providers (such as therapists) who are employed by a corporation or foundation that principally provides professional services within the scope of the TRICARE benefit. A participation agreement is required before entities approved under this provision may bill TRICARE for their services. Following the principle that secondary payments will be made only if services are payable by TRICARE leads to the conclusion that TRICARE will not cover services furnished by CORFs and OPTs in the absence of a participation agreement. Unless this policy is changed, this situation is likely to become a source of beneficiary confusion and misunderstanding.

Another area in which the two programs diverge is speech-language pathology. Under Medicare, services of speech-language pathologists in independent practice are not covered. TRICARE covers these services if a physician refers the beneficiary for treatment and provides continuing and ongoing oversight and supervision. TRICARE's coverage of services provided by audiologists in independent practice is also less restrictive than Medicare's. Medicare will pay for only diagnostic tests, whereas TRICARE will cover other services prescribed by a physician so long as they are part of a treatment addressing a physical defect and not an educational or occupational deficit (in which educational or vocational training rather than medical care is needed to remedy the problem).

Medicare requires a patient visit to a physician at least every 30 days to satisfy the requirement for physician oversight of the plan of treatment for care provided by an occupational or physical therapist. While TRICARE requires continuing and ongoing oversight of the treatment, national policies regarding the frequency of physician visits have not been established. If the TFL beneficiary does not have the Medicare-required visits, Medicare will not pay for the therapy services. It appears that TRICARE will become the primary payer and the beneficiary will be responsible for coinsurance amounts.

Coverage for Cardiac Rehabilitation
Differences in how Medicare and TRICARE cover cardiac rehabilitation services illustrate how varying coverage limits and policies can cause potential difficulties in understanding of benefits and processing claims.

Medicare covers supervised cardiac rehabilitation as a physician service. The current Medicare policy covers physician-supervised cardiac rehabilitation for patients who (1) have a documented diagnosis of acute myocardial infarction within the preceding 12 months; or (2) have had coronary bypass surgery; and/or (3) have stable angina pectoris. CMS is evaluating whether to expand coverage for the following additional indications: (1) heart valve replacement; (2) angioplasty; (3) heart or heart-lung transplant; and (4) congestive heart failure.

---

[13] The Balanced Budget Act of 1997 imposed a $1,500 cap on the combined total of physical therapy and speech-language pathology services furnished in a calendar year and a separate $1,500 cap on occupational therapy. The $1,500 cap did not apply to services furnished by a hospital outpatient department. Subsequent legislation suspended the cap effective January 1, 2000, through calendar year 2002.

TRICARE currently covers cardiac rehabilitation following angioplasty in addition to the three conditions Medicare currently covers. Until Medicare expands the indications for this care, Medicare denials for cardiac rehabilitation following angioplasty probably will cite no "medical necessity" as the reason. If so, this is an illustration of a case when a Medicare "medical necessity" denial will trigger a TRICARE denial for a service it normally covers.

TRICARE requires that the cardiac rehabilitation be provided by a CHAMPUS-authorized hospital. Medicare allows freestanding physician-directed cardiac rehabilitation facilities to provide the services. Medicare is assessing whether physician supervision is required (if it is not, a legislative change would be required to cover it as a non-physician benefit). This is another example of when differences in the providers who are authorized to provide a service could lead to confusion and misunderstanding for the beneficiary.

Comparison of Coverage for Behavioral Health Services

Table 2.4 summarizes the behavioral health benefits provided under Medicare and TRICARE. Both programs have medical review guidelines that limit benefits for some types of behavioral health services (for both mental and substance use disorders), including both inpatient and outpatient services. These benefits can be increased if additional services are determined to be medically necessary. The Medicare 190-day lifetime limit on inpatient care provided by psychiatric hospitals is established by law and cannot be waived.

As the discussions in the following sections illustrate, important issues to consider are the complexity of these differences in benefits and the potential difficulty beneficiaries face trying to make sense of them and to coordinate them in a time of crisis. In particular, beneficiaries in need of mental health care may have difficulty understanding their benefits due to impaired cognition. While TRICARE has indicated that beneficiaries will be protected and benefits extended if utilization management (UM) parameters are met, beneficiaries and their families bear the ultimate responsibility for understanding how these benefits will work together to cover care in a time of crisis. The adequacy of the benefits provided by the two programs is a different issue that is beyond the scope of this study.

Inpatient Services

Under TRICARE, payment for inpatient psychiatric care is limited to 30 days per fiscal year. The limitation is required by statute, but a waiver may be obtained for medically necessary care beyond 30 days.[14] Therefore, TRICARE payments for TFL beneficiaries' deductibles or coinsurance beyond day 30 will be contingent upon waiver of the 30-day limit under TRICARE.

TRICARE requires that inpatient stays for psychiatric care be preauthorized. If an institutional provider fails to obtain preauthorization, TRICARE benefits will be extended; however, a penalty of not less than 10 percent will be applied.[15] This requirement also used

---

[14] Public Law 101-510 and 101-511, 32 CFR 199.4, July 2001.

[15] 32 CFR 199.15. TRICARE has indicated in a letter to a managed health care company that this penalty will be applied when inpatient admissions are not preauthorized according to TRICARE policy. Capt. John D'Alessandro, chief, Managed

Table 2.4
Behavioral Health Benefits

Benefit Type	Medicare	TRICARE
Mental Health Services		
Inpatient hospital services	General Hospital—Same as other inpatient hospital benefits (150 days per benefit period plus 60 days lifetime reserve) Psychiatric Hospital—190-day lifetime limit	30-day limit per fiscal year or 30 days per admission;[a] preauthorization required
Outpatient services	50% coinsurance for visits to qualified providers for psychotherapy and medication management; 80% coinsurance for brief office visits to psychiatrists for monitoring or changing psychotropic medication, psychiatric evaluation, and/or consultation No case identification or case management and no prescription drug benefit	20% coinsurance for visits to qualified providers; limited to two visits per week; individual psychotherapy sessions limited to 60 minutes and family sessions to 90 minutes; more than eight psychotherapy visits must be preauthorized [b] Prescription drug benefit
Partial hospitalization	20% coinsurance; no day limits	Limited to 60 treatment days in benefit period; preauthorization required
Residential treatment	Not covered	150-day limit; preauthorization required
Substance Abuse Services (Alcohol and Drug)		
Lifetime treatment limit	None	Limited to three benefit periods for any substance disorder treatment in a lifetime[c]
Inpatient detoxification	Alcohol—National guidelines cover five days Drug—Local medical review policies	7 days covered; $20 per day copayment
Inpatient rehabilitation	Alcohol—National guidelines cover 16–19 days Drug—Local medical review policies	21 days covered; $20 per day copayment
Outpatient	50% coinsurance; diagnostic and therapeutic services covered; educational and family services covered if directly related to treatment	20% coinsurance; limited to 60 group visits in benefit period, and 15 days family visits in benefit period
Partial hospitalization	Same as mental health	Same as mental health
Residential treatment	Not covered	Admission to a residential treatment center primarily for substance abuse rehabilitation not covered

[a] TRICARE allows 45 days annually for children and adolescents. This limit can be increased by a waiver if the care is documented as being medically necessary.

[b] Outpatient psychotherapy visits can be preauthorized in clusters of eight visits at a time. MCSC variation exists in how these visits are preauthorized.

[c] TRICARE definition: A benefit period that starts with the first date of covered treatment and ends 365 days later, regardless of the total services actually used within the benefit period.

Care Support Office, letter to Charles Rose, vice president, Government Contracts, Health Net Federal Services, Inc., August 14, 2001.

to apply to TFL beneficiary stays; i.e., hospitals were required to seek preauthorization for all TFL beneficiaries who were admitted for inpatient psychiatric care in order to receive payment to cover the beneficiary's deductible.[16] Section 701 of the FY2003 NDAA (Public Law 107-314) eliminated the preauthorization requirement effective October 2003 for TFL beneficiary stays that are covered by Medicare Part A benefits. If Part A benefits become no longer payable, preauthorization will be required for TRICARE coverage for the continued stay. Once a beneficiary exceeds his or her Medicare lifetime limit on psychiatric hospitalization, standard TRICARE cost-sharing rules will apply for any future inpatient admissions for care that is preauthorized, within TRICARE limits, and meets TRICARE UM parameters.

Outpatient Care

For outpatient services under Medicare Part B, Medicare provides only 50 percent coinsurance for mental health and substance abuse services rendered by qualified providers.[17] However, brief medication management (i.e., Current Procedure Terminology (CPT) code 90862) and psychiatric diagnosis and evaluation are covered at 80 percent. TRICARE covers 80 percent of most outpatient mental health services (including psychotherapy) provided by qualified providers[18] but imposes some restrictions on the frequency and length of visits to be covered. For example, preauthorization is required for more than eight psychotherapy visits. Up to eight additional psychotherapy visits can be preauthorized at a time if deemed necessary by the contractor; however, some variation exists among MCSCs in how these visits are preauthorized. TRICARE staff has indicated that carriers will not impose the preauthorization requirement for psychotherapy visits that exceed their current limits for the TFL beneficiaries (i.e., more than eight psychotherapy visits).[19] For TFL beneficiaries, TRICARE has indicated that it will process all claims for outpatient psychotherapy as a secondary payer provided Medicare covers the services as being medically necessary. This relaxed policy by default provides TFL beneficiaries with unlimited access to medically necessary outpatient psychiatric treatment that will be covered 50 percent by Medicare and 50 percent by TRICARE.

TRICARE also provides TFL beneficiaries with pharmacy benefits;[20] however, the TRICARE pharmacy benefit lacks limits imposed by the standard Medigap plans. TFL beneficiaries will face nominal copayments for psychotropic medications depending on the type of drug (generic versus brand name) and on the mode of prescription fulfillment (MTF, mail order pharmacy, network retail pharmacy, or non-network retail pharmacy). Therefore, TFL beneficiaries not only will have free unlimited access to psychotherapy but will also have access to affordable and effective psychotropic medications.

---

[16] By law (Public Law 99-514), Medicare institutional providers must accept TRICARE for institutional services.

[17] Qualified providers of mental health and substance abuse services under Medicare include psychiatrists, clinical psychologists, clinical social workers, clinical nurse specialists, nurse practitioners, and physician's assistants (Health Care Financing Administration, 2000).

[18] Qualified providers of mental health and substance abuse services under TRICARE include psychiatrists, certified clinical social workers, certified psychiatric nurse specialists, clinical psychologists, certified marriage and family therapists, pastoral counselors, and mental health counselors (TRICARE/CHAMPUS Policy Manual 6010.47-M, 1999, Chapter 10). Unlike Medicare, TRICARE includes marriage and family therapists and pastoral and mental health counselors.

[19] Personal communication, TMA operations staff Aurora, Colorado, July 25, 2001.

[20] The TRICARE Senior Pharmacy was implemented on April 1, 2001, and extends pharmacy benefits to all military retirees 65 or older.

TFL decreases the financial barriers to outpatient mental health services for the dually eligible population. In general, Medicare's benefits are more expansive. Because the "soft" restriction requiring preauthorization for more than eight outpatient psychotherapy visits will not be required under TFL,[21] beneficiaries have fewer financial disincentives to limit their utilization. It will be important for TMA and Medicare to monitor trends in utilization to determine the impact of providing basically free, unlimited outpatient mental health care. It may also be important for DoD to understand how changing the patient cost for provider services relative to medication costs impacts service utilization and quality of care.

Partial Hospitalization

Partial hospitalization[22] is covered under Medicare with only a 20 percent coinsurance and no lifetime limit. TRICARE requires that all partial hospitalizations be preauthorized, occur within a TRICARE-certified partial hospital setting, and be limited to 60 treatment days in a fiscal year. Therefore, if partial hospitalization is preauthorized, TRICARE will cover the 20 percent coinsurance for partial hospitalization (in a TRICARE certified partial hospitalization program) up to 60 days in a benefit period. Beyond 60 days, the beneficiary will be responsible for the 20 percent coinsurance under Medicare. Again, TRICARE will not cost-share unless the partial hospitalization care is rendered in a TRICARE qualified program. It is important to note that, as of this writing, it is not clear whether the relaxed policy for preauthorization for inpatient psychiatric admissions will also apply to partial hospitalization.

Substance Abuse Treatment

Medicare and TRICARE have similar coverage policies for inpatient substance (alcohol and drug) abuse services, including detoxification and rehabilitation. Medicare typically pays 100 percent of medically necessary inpatient hospital services (after the Part A deductible has been satisfied), whereas TRICARE requires a $20 per day copayment. If medically necessary inpatient care for substance abuse disorders remain within Medicare's benefit period limits, TRICARE will have limited (e.g., for the beneficiary's Medicare deductible) or no liability for cost-sharing.

In addition, Medicare covers outpatient services for substance abuse disorders at 50 percent (similar to Medicare coverage for mental health services) with no preestablished limits on frequency. TRICARE, on the other hand, limits the frequency of outpatient group and family visits within a benefit period. At the time of this writing, TRICARE has not indicated that it would relax this limit for substance abuse treatment (as it did for outpatient mental health visits).

In considering coverage for TFL beneficiaries seeking care for substance abuse, some important complexities are noted. First, TRICARE limits coverage for both inpatient and outpatient substance abuse services to three benefit periods in a lifetime. As such, it is possible that if a beneficiary seeks services even only once per year, he or she will exhaust his or her TRICARE coverage for substance abuse care within three years. Second, TRICARE de-

---

[21] Personal communication with TMA operations staff, Aurora, Colorado, July 25, 2001.

[22] Partial hospitalization is defined as a structured program of active treatment that is more intense than the care received in a doctor's or therapist's office and that is given through hospital outpatient departments and local community mental health centers (Health Care Financing Administration, 2000).

fines "benefit period" differently than Medicare does. Under Medicare, a benefit period begins with an initial hospitalization and ends when the beneficiary has not received hospital or skilled nursing care for 60 days in a row. Under TRICARE, a benefit period is defined as 365 days from the first date of services. These differences could have complex implications for how Medicare and TRICARE work together to cover substance abuse treatment within a given episode of care.

Given these differing definitions as well as the TRICARE lifetime limit, TRICARE's liability for the costs of substance abuse treatment services provided to TFL beneficiaries will depend on the date of service within both the Medicare and TRICARE defined benefit period (rather than just the Medicare period as is the case for most if not all other types of medical services) and whether or not the beneficiary has reached the TRICARE lifetime limit. It is unclear how these differences will be recognized and handled during the claims adjudication process, and it is likely that they will result in confusion on the part of the beneficiary and provider. At the time of this writing, it is unclear whether use of Medicare covered services for substance abuse disorders will trigger a TRICARE benefit period (to which the beneficiary is limited to three in a lifetime) and would impact TRICARE's coverage of the inpatient deductible beyond three TRICARE benefit periods.

Potential Changes to Medicare Benefits for Behavioral Health Care

TFL's liability for mental health benefits is likely to change if Medicare's benefits change. For instance, the proposed Medicare Mental Health Modernization Act of 2001 (S. 690/H.R. 1522) sought to establish parity for mental health benefits covered under Medicare, expand coverage for community-based services, and increase access to Medicare-covered services. Assuming TFL policies did not change, several provisions of this proposed legislation would have lowered TFL's liability for costs associated with mental health coverage. The most obvious example is the parity provision, which would lower Medicare's mental health coinsurance rate from 50 percent to 20 percent. Expanding the types of intensive outpatient services covered under Medicare might also lower TFL's costs, to the extent that such services are already covered by TRICARE.

The parity bill also proposed extending direct reimbursement to qualified (state-licensed) mental health counselors and marriage and family therapists for services provided to Medicare beneficiaries. While TRICARE does not provide coverage for marriage or family counseling, it does provide reimbursement for psychotherapy or counseling services for the treatment of a mental disorder provided by qualified mental health counselors and/or marriage and family therapists, with a 20 percent coinsurance rate.

Similarly, the bill sought to allow clinical social workers to bill directly for mental health (diagnostic and therapeutic) services provided to residents of SNFs and aimed to disentangle these types of services from the social/case management types of "social services" provided in SNFs (e.g., identification of other eligible programs for beneficiaries, such as Medicaid, and coordination of benefits).[23] Medicare currently includes these services in its

---

[23] Currently under TRICARE, clinical social workers are allowed to bill directly for mental health services provided in SNFs. As we discussed earlier in this section, TMA should examine existing policies regarding mental health services provided to SNF residents by clinical social workers to ensure that double payments are not made (since their costs would currently be covered by the Medicare payment, but are also billable under TRICARE).

per diem rate. Under the proposed legislation, the services would have been separately billable to Medicare as the primary payer and TRICARE as the secondary payer.

Conclusions and Recommendations

Most health care services that are covered benefits under TRICARE are also covered benefits under Medicare, and vice versa. However, because TFL benefits are based on the existing TRICARE program, they were not expressly designed to fit together with those of Medicare (in contrast to privately purchased Medicare supplemental or "Medigap" policies). As a result, certain benefit and coverage inconsistencies pose operational challenges and are likely to lead to confusion and misunderstanding for beneficiaries. The legislative changes in the FY2002 NDAA, which made TRICARE coverage and payment policies for SNF and HHA services conform with Medicare's policies, addressed the most problematic area. The changes in the FY2003 NDAA to eliminate the requirement for prior authorization for mental health inpatient hospital services and to provide that Medicare-approved providers are also approved to provide services under TFL should further reduce the administrative burden and confusion.

A potential issue for TFL is whether the coding specificity in Medicare's claims determination is sufficient for TRICARE to distinguish between Medicare coverage and medical necessity determinations, establish its cost-sharing liability accurately, and afford the beneficiary sufficient appeal rights. This issue is of particular concern for emerging technologies for which TRICARE and Medicare have different coverage policies. We believe that TFL will highlight coverage inconsistencies between TRICARE and Medicare and may create pressure for consistent "federal" coverage policy. As a general rule, there should be a clear rationale for why a specific technology is covered by one program and not the other.

To conclude this chapter, we offer the following recommendations and related discussion:

- Claims for services for which Medicare and TRICARE coverage policies diverge should be reviewed to assure that the claims adjudication and appeals processes for TFL beneficiaries are working as intended.
- TMA should participate in the CMS MCAC deliberations.

Provisions in the FY2002 NDAA to make TRICARE SNF and HHA benefits conform to Medicare's coverage and payment policies should eliminate many of the coordination of benefit issues that otherwise would have occurred for post-acute care services. Remaining areas of potential concern for DoD include the lack of (1) any limitation on the duration of SNF benefits, and (2) any TFL enhancements for HHA care. If there is a significant volume of continued SNF stays, another potential issue may be taking advantage of Medicare Part B coverage for services furnished to SNF inpatients whose SNF stay is not covered by Medicare Part A.

Expanded home health benefits could reduce extended SNF stays and expand TFL beneficiary care choices. TRICARE could supplement Medicare-covered home health benefits so that a beneficiary who requires more than intermittent skilled nursing care could obtain coverage for intermittent part-time care from both Medicare and TRICARE (i.e., in total, the TFL beneficiary could be covered for up to 56 hours of skilled nursing care per week). The expanded home health benefit could be offered to all TFL beneficiaries or only to those beneficiaries who would otherwise qualify for continuing skilled nursing facility care, (e.g., those who require daily skilled nursing care or skilled rehabilitative care five times per week). In this case, TRICARE's payment could be limited to what its liability would be for SNF care (the Medicare coinsurance amount or 75 percent of the per diem rate) and continue only so long as the beneficiary continued to need an SNF level of care.

- The use of post-acute care services by TFL beneficiaries should be monitored. Particular attention should be paid to beneficiaries with continued SNF stays after their Medicare SNF benefits have been exhausted. If there is a significant incidence of continued SNF stays, a study of the cost effectiveness of expanded home health benefits would be warranted.

The differences in Medicare and TRICARE coverage policies for behavioral health services make it likely that beneficiaries will find this area of their health coverage relatively confusing, even with the TRICARE preauthorization requirement for inpatient psychiatric care covered by Medicare Part A benefits, which became effective October 1, 2003. TRICARE's lifetime limit of three benefit periods for the coverage of substance abuse treatment services may remain problematic. Because TRICARE and Medicare define benefit periods differently and TRICARE's liability for Medicare Part A covered stays may be minimal, the determination of when and how the TRICARE limit is reached is likely to be somewhat complex and confusing to both providers and beneficiaries. With regard to outpatient mental health services, TFL beneficiaries have unlimited access to medically necessary psychiatric treatment and few financial incentives to limit care.

- DoD should examine and consider the impact of removing the three-benefit-period limit on substance abuse benefits for the TFL population.
- DoD should conduct a close examination of mental health service utilization and costs to determine the impact of providing what is essentially free unlimited care for outpatient mental health. This examination should be conducted across the direct and purchased care systems. With regard to the TFL population, several studies are available that estimate the need for, utilization of, and costs associated with mental health services in the elderly population;[24] however, it is unclear how the costs relate to or compare with the military retiree population, and, in turn, what the costs to DoD might be under TFL.

In undertaking such a study, we recommend that DoD consider using both narrow and broad definitions of mental health service use. It would be important to consider health care services using all connected domains of delivery: where, what, by whom, for whom, and how much. It would also be necessary to understand and adjust for any differences in how Medicare and TRICARE classify and code claims as either mental health service claims or not (based on diagnosis or procedure, or both). Such information and data would allow

---

[24] See, for example, Himelhoch et al., 2004, pp. 512–521.

DoD to consider the impact on its liability for mental health services furnished to the TFL population and to estimate the cost of eliminating for TFL beneficiaries the benefit period limits for substance use treatment benefits.

CHAPTER THREE

TRICARE for Life Beneficiary Cost-Sharing for Civilian Care

The FY2001 NDAA directed the Department of Defense to implement TRICARE for Life without premiums, deductibles, or copayments for beneficiaries. Beneficiaries are required only to enroll in Medicare Part B as a condition of TFL participation. TFL beneficiaries do incur out-of-pocket costs for using services that are not covered by Medicare, including outpatient prescription drugs; for such services that are covered by TRICARE, beneficiaries pay the standard TRICARE out-of-pocket costs.

In this chapter, we consider the potential consequences for DoD, for Medicare, and for beneficiaries of the current TFL cost-sharing policy for civilian care relative to the status quo prior to the introduction of TFL, and the potential benefits and costs for these stakeholders from alternative cost-sharing policies.

Coverage and Premiums Prior to TRICARE for Life

Many Medicare beneficiaries, including Medicare-eligible military retirees, have health insurance coverage that supplements Medicare. They obtain this coverage from a variety of sources, including private Medicare supplemental plans (commonly referred to as "Medigap" plans), plans sponsored by former (or, for those who are working, current) employers, Medicare Health Maintenance Organizations (HMOs), Medicaid, and/or other public programs.

Private Medigap plans are standardized, with ten different benefit packages.[1] All of these Medigap plans eliminate Medicare's coinsurance for inpatient care under Medicare Part A and outpatient care under Part B. In general, they also reduce or eliminate out-of-pocket costs for other Medicare-covered services (with the types of services varying by plan), extend Medicare's benefit limits for certain services, and cover some services—particularly prescription drugs—that Medicare does not cover. Employer-sponsored supplemental plans serve similar functions. However, because such plans are most commonly designed to mirror the benefits offered to active employees, they generally include modest cost-sharing requirements, although they are lower than Medicare's similar requirements. At the same time, employer-sponsored plans generally include more comprehensive coverage for prescription drugs than do private Medigap plans (U.S. General Accounting Office, 2001a, 2001b; Laschober et al., 2002).

In addition, some Medicare beneficiaries enroll in HMOs under the Medicare+Choice program. Such plans reduce out-of-pocket expenses relative to fee-for-service Medicare and

---

[1] These plans are referenced by the consecutive letters A through J.

they may offer additional benefits, such as transportation, eye glasses, coordination of care, or prescription drugs. Premiums for Medicare+Choice plans tend to be substantially lower than those for Medigap plans. In recent years, many Medicare HMOs have withdrawn from the market. While most Medicare beneficiaries living in urban areas continue to have a Medicare HMO option, many beneficiaries in less-urban or rural areas are not served by a Medicare HMO. Furthermore, even where Medicare HMOs remain available, the relative generosity of their benefits has decreased and the out-of-pocket costs for members have increased (e.g., Kaiser Family Foundation, 1999; Grossman et al., 2002). Private Medigap plans require beneficiaries to pay premiums, which vary by type of plan and, for most beneficiaries who enroll after age 65, by age and/or health status. Only three of the ten standardized Medigap policies include any prescription drug coverage; two of these currently have an annual benefit limit of $1,250 and the third has an annual limit of $3,000. Prior to the institution of TFL, affinity organizations such as The Retired Officers Association offered basic Medigap plans to military retirees without medical underwriting; however, these offerings are limited to plans A through F, i.e., those without any prescription drug coverage. Employer-sponsored Medigap plans may also require premiums, but this varies by employer.[2] Medicare HMOs may also require premiums, which vary by plan.

Prevalence of Supplemental Coverage Prior to TRICARE for Life

We know of no definitive information on the prevalence of Medicare supplemental coverage or Medicare+Choice enrollment among DoD beneficiaries who are eligible for TFL.[3] Data on the general Medicare population, however, suggest that relatively few Medicare beneficiaries have only Medicare (see Table 3.1). For instance, the majority of Medicare beneficiaries whose income is above the poverty line have private supplemental insurance, via either a former employer or a Medigap policy. Roughly 11 percent have only Medicare. However, Table 3.1 does not address the case of Medicare-eligible military retirees who live in the catchment areas of MTFs and receive care there; such care is provided at no charge to the beneficiary on a space-available basis.

Data from RAND's evaluation of the TRICARE Senior Prime Demonstration suggest that similar fractions of military retirees and other Medicare beneficiaries, respectively, were enrolled in Medicare+Choice plans in demonstration catchment areas prior to the demonstration.[4] It seems plausible that the fraction of military retirees who are covered by employer/retiree benefits may be lower than the fraction of civilian Medicare beneficiaries due to their differing work histories (i.e., career employment with an employer, DoD, that did not offer such coverage prior to TFL).

---

[2] U.S. General Accounting Office, 2001b.

[3] The TMA is currently collecting such data as part of its ongoing beneficiary surveys.

[4] Schoenbaum et al., 2002.

Table 3.1
Health Insurance of Medicare Beneficiaries Age 65 or Over, by Income Level, 1997

Insurance	All Beneficiaries (%)	Income at <100% of Federal Poverty Level (%)	Income at 100%–200% of Federal Poverty Level (%)	Income at >200% of Federal Poverty Level (%)
Employer/retiree	35	8	26	50
Medigap	25	15	28	27
Public	2	3	3	1
Medicare HMO	14	6	16	16
Medicaid	14	52	13	1
Medicare only	10	16	14	5

NOTES: Columns may not sum to 100% due to rounding. Employer/retiree includes beneficiaries who have supplemental insurance from a former employer or union and beneficiaries who are still working and whose employer is their primary source of insurance.

SOURCE: Urban Institute analyses of the 1997 Medicare Current Beneficiary Survey, cited in Kaiser Family Foundation, 2001.

Potential Consequences of TFL Cost-Sharing for Beneficiaries

Beneficiaries who paid premiums for private Medigap or employer-sponsored retiree benefits will save those premium amounts if they replace their private coverage with TFL. This benefit may be substantial, particularly for beneficiaries with preexisting medical conditions who are interested in prescription drug coverage.[5] At the same time, military retirees who were not previously enrolled in Medicare Part B will need to enroll as a condition of participation in TFL. For those who are over 65, their annual Part B premium will be increased by 10 percent each year they were not enrolled since age 65.[6]

Beneficiaries who faced cost-sharing provisions under various supplemental insurance policies—or, most significantly, under Medicare with no supplemental insurance—will face little or no cost-sharing under the current policy. In particular, they will face no deductibles, copayments, or coinsurance for Medicare-covered services; they will have TRICARE copayments for services that are not covered by Medicare but are covered by TRICARE.

The reduction or elimination of cost-sharing provisions reduces the chance that beneficiaries will defer or forgo needed medical care for financial reasons, and this may improve the health, financial well-being, and quality of life for some beneficiaries. However, available evidence from the Health Insurance Experiment (HIE) suggests that modest cost-sharing provisions have little or no effect on health status, relative to free care, except for poor patients with certain chronic medical conditions.[7] Furthermore, the HIE investigators reported that

---

[5] Among non-institutionalized Medicare beneficiaries age 65 or over, those with private Medigap spent an average of $1,360 in Medigap premiums in 1999 (American Association of Retired People, 1999). Data from 2000 on the average annual premiums for Medigap plans indicate that the national average premiums for plans with prescription drug benefits were $2,347 (Plan H), $2,423 (Plan I), and $3,065 (Plan J) (Weiss Ratings, 2000).

[6] A RAND evaluation of TRICARE Senior Prime reported that approximately 7 percent of eligible beneficiaries in demonstration catchment areas were enrolled in Part A only (Farley et al., 2000 and 2003).

[7] See, e.g., Newhouse and the Insurance Experiment Group, 1993; Manning et al., 1987; Brook et al., 1983 and 1984.

targeted programs aimed at hypertension and other chronic conditions were likely to be much more cost-effective methods for improving health status than free care for all services.[8]

TFL beneficiaries will also be covered by TRICARE's stop-loss provision, which caps beneficiaries' out-of-pocket spending for TRICARE-covered services at a set amount (currently $3,000) and covers 100 percent of covered costs above that amount. Private Medigap plans do not currently have such a provision; the existence and level of stop-loss provisions in employer/retiree plans and other sorts of supplemental coverage vary by plan. It is not known how many TFL beneficiaries are likely to reach the stop-loss provision,[9] but for those who do, its value may be quite substantial, representing true insurance against catastrophic loss.

Potential Consequences of TFL Cost-Sharing for the Department of Defense

TFL represents a new financial outlay for DoD, in the sense that DoD offered no explicit Medicare supplemental insurance prior to the provisions in the FY2001 NDAA. However, the magnitude of this outlay is likely to be affected in several ways by TFL's cost-sharing policies. One effect is the level of TFL participation. As it is currently designed, it seems likely that nearly all eligible beneficiaries with private supplemental coverage will replace that coverage with TFL because TFL has very comprehensive benefits, no premiums, and few or no cost-sharing requirements. (Technically, such private coverage would apply before TFL, for beneficiaries who have both; however, beneficiaries are not required to maintain private coverage as a condition of TFL participation.)

For the same reasons, and because participation requires no means test and is not socially stigmatized, TFL is likely to replace other public supplemental coverage for some of those TFL beneficiaries who would otherwise receive public coverage.[10] Beneficiaries may simply not bother to apply for public coverage when they are eligible for TFL unless they need long-term care or other services that are not covered by TRICARE. Thus, the fraction of eligible beneficiaries who participate in TFL is likely to be high.

At the same time, the generosity of TFL may reduce the demand for MTF services, which DoD currently funds in its entirety. Issues related to managing MTF care are discussed in Chapter Four and cost issues are discussed in Chapter Five.

While the FY2001 NDAA precludes the use of deductibles and copayments, it may be worth considering the consequences of implementing modest cost-sharing provisions for Medicare-covered services (e.g., similar to current TRICARE copayments). First, such provisions might reduce participation in TFL somewhat, relative to the current program, and it

---

[8] Because the HIE was a randomized control trial, the results are generally unaffected by patient self-selection and similar factors that would otherwise bias results. However, there are a number of reasons why the HIE results may not be definitive in this setting, including that it was conducted 20 years ago, in relatively few locations (six), and among a non-aged population rather than among Medicare beneficiaries. Evidence on the price-elasticity of demand for medical care is reviewed in Ringel et al., 2002.

[9] Available data on non-institutionalized Medicare beneficiaries age 65 or over regarding out-of-pocket spending on premiums (Part B and supplemental) and medical care in 1999 indicate that 11 percent spent between $3,000 and $4,000 out-of-pocket, 6 percent between $4,000 and $5,000, and 8 percent more than $5,000 (American Association of Retired People, 1999). Considering that average spending on insurance premiums—which do not count toward out-of-pocket maximums—is between $500 and $2,000, it suggests that relatively few Medicare beneficiaries currently exceed $3,000 in annual out-of-pocket spending for medical care.

[10] TRICARE is primary to Medicaid for TRICARE-covered services.

might reduce DoD's costs in several other ways. Most obviously, for a given pattern of health care use, cost-sharing provisions such as copayments would shift some cost from the current payers to the beneficiaries. Second, such cost-sharing provisions have been shown to reduce health care use, while being unlikely to affect health status significantly. Third, while TFL beneficiaries currently face no cost-sharing for most types of medical services, they do have copayments for prescription drugs under DoD's pharmacy benefit program (except for prescriptions filled at MTF pharmacies). Relative to a policy with modest cost-sharing for Medicare-covered services, this sort of policy may reduce patient demand for medications and increase demand for other types of care (particularly physician services) in ways that may not be cost-effective for DoD or the federal government.[11]

Potential Consequences of TFL Cost-Sharing for Medicare

TFL is likely to increase Medicare spending for covered beneficiaries for several reasons. It is possible, if not likely, that TFL will reduce demand for MTF services because one of the things that is appealing about MTF care—that it involves no out-of-pocket costs—now applies to Medicare-covered services provided in the community as well. By statute, Medicare is currently prohibited from reimbursing MTFs for care provided to Medicare-eligible beneficiaries; therefore, such substitution away from MTF care increases Medicare outlays. This issue is discussed in further detail in Chapter Five.

More significantly, beneficiaries will face the same or lower cost-sharing for Medicare-covered services under TFL than the cost-sharing under their previous insurance coverage. To the extent that cost-sharing is lower, health care use is likely to increase relative to the status quo, with corresponding increases in Medicare outlays. In the HIE, for instance, total annual health care spending was 22 percent higher under a plan with no cost-sharing than under a plan with 25 percent coinsurance, a level that is similar to the cost-sharing for outpatient care under Medicare for beneficiaries without any supplemental coverage.[12]

Furthermore, TFL and DoD's new pharmacy benefit program is very likely to reduce demand for Medicare+Choice HMOs by military retirees because the enhanced benefits that have made these plans relatively attractive are now available from DoD.[13] In the HIE, total annual spending was 20 percent higher under a plan with no cost-sharing than under an HMO plan, although these effects were for a non-aged population rather than for Medicare beneficiaries, and the HMO was not specifically a Medicare+Choice plan.[14] Further research is needed to assess the change in health care costs by TFL beneficiaries in standard Medicare (plus TFL), relative to those in a Medicare+Choice plan.

At the same time, DoD's pharmacy benefit program significantly improves access to prescription drugs for many beneficiaries, who previously had limited or no insurance coverage for prescription drugs. Relative to the status quo, this increased access has ambiguous ef-

---

[11] The new formulary system that DoD is currently developing is intended to minimize such problems by considering the cost to DoD and cost-effectiveness in determining copayments.

[12] Manning et al., 1987.

[13] Also, as noted above, Medicare HMOs have been offering fewer and less generous benefits beyond those that are required by Medicare, further enhancing the relative appeal of TFL for affected beneficiaries.

[14] Manning et al., 1987.

fects on Medicare outlays. On the one hand, prescription drugs may serve as relatively cost-effective substitutes for other types of care. On the other hand, improved access to medications may be associated with generally higher health care use, e.g., if patients visit providers to obtain prescriptions and manage their medications. Also, for beneficiaries with prior pharmacy coverage, TFL may change their relative costs for prescription drugs and other services and thus their demand for those services, as discussed above.

Relative to TFL's current cost-sharing policies, modest cost-sharing provisions for Medicare-covered services would be likely to reduce the cost to Medicare of providing health benefits by reducing demand for civilian health care services.

Potential Consequences of TFL Cost-Sharing for Taxpayers

Relative to the status quo prior to the FY2001 NDAA, TFL benefits will clearly increase federal expenditures for military retirees. In addition to the impact of the TFL benefit per se, the absence of cost-sharing under TFL will increase demand for Medicare-covered services, increasing Medicare outlays.

Relative to TFL's current cost-sharing policies, modest cost-sharing provisions for Medicare-covered services would be likely to reduce health care use, and thus federal expenditures under both TFL and Medicare. Such provisions would also be likely to change the relative demand for medical services and the demand for prescription drugs under the DoD's pharmacy benefit program in ways that may be cost-effective from the perspective of federal taxpayers.

Finally, modest cost-sharing might reduce participation in TFL somewhat. It might also increase demand for space-available MTF care by TFL beneficiaries. Whether such a shift would be cost-effective from the perspective of federal taxpayers is discussed further in Chapter Five.

Conclusions and Recommendations

As specified in the FY2001 NDAA, TFL is being implemented without premiums, deductibles, or copayments. Compared with the health insurance options previously available to Medicare-eligible military retirees, TFL is likely to be of substantially greater value to most beneficiaries, with few or no drawbacks. At the same time, TFL will substantially increase federal spending—both because of the new benefits *per se* and because the absence of cost-sharing is likely to increase health care use because beneficiaries no longer have cost-sharing as an incentive to use less care. Our recommendations focus primarily on this latter effect.

In our view, DoD and Medicare are likely to benefit if modest cost-sharing were introduced into TFL—for instance, such as the cost-sharing that military retirees under age 65 currently have under TRICARE Prime. Some amount of cost-sharing by beneficiaries is nearly universal in private group health insurance plans, including employer-sponsored retiree plans (Kaiser Family Foundation, 2002). For Medicare beneficiaries, supplemental coverage with modest cost-sharing substantially reduces the out-of-pocket costs that would arise under the standard Medicare benefit, while retaining some modest incentives to control health care use and costs.

By "modest" cost-sharing provisions, we envision primarily fixed-dollar copayments, on the order of $10 per visit, for ambulatory care visits. Such copayments are similar in form and magnitude to those required in many employer-sponsored supplemental plans and Medicare+Choice HMOs (and in TRICARE for military retirees under 65). They are also similar to the copayments currently required under DoD's pharmacy benefit program. Fixed-dollar copayments have the advantage of being easy to understand because they are independent of the actual billed or Medicare-covered charge. They are also easy to administer; in many private plans, for instance, beneficiaries pay the copayment at the time of service, with no additional paperwork.

All else being equal, the introduction of cost-sharing in TFL would be likely to reduce the cost of the program to the federal government. However, this change could be made revenue-neutral by applying the resulting savings toward other benefits for the covered population—such as enhanced coverage for post-acute care services (see Chapter Two) or long-term care services, or a reduction in the current TFL out-of-pocket maximum—thereby potentially increasing the overall value of the TFL benefit.[15] Further research into the preferences of TFL beneficiaries and the likely consequences of introducing cost-sharing (versus free care) in TFL would help identify strategies to maximize the overall value of the TFL benefit.

---

[15] In general, such changes would increase the value of TFL for some beneficiaries (e.g., those who reach the out-of-pocket maximum, or who value access to long-term care services) and decrease it for others (e.g., those who place relatively high value on an insurance benefit with no cost-sharing).

CHAPTER FOUR

Managing Military Treatment Facility Care Provided to TRICARE for Life Beneficiaries

This chapter examines several issues surrounding the desirability and feasibility of managed care options for Medicare-eligible military retirees.[1] We focus primarily on the new TRICARE Plus program because it is being implemented alongside TFL and because current statutes effectively preclude DoD from mandating most aspects of managed care for Medicare-covered services under TFL.

Medicare is primarily an unmanaged benefit, in the sense that there are very few restrictions on where, when, or what type of health care Medicare beneficiaries can get (for covered services). This aspect of Medicare, combined with the absence of cost-sharing for Medicare-covered services under TFL, differentiates Medicare from nearly every other private group health plan, including employer-sponsored retiree programs (and TRICARE for military retirees under age 65) (Kaiser Family Foundation, 2002).

As discussed in Chapter Three, TFL is likely to draw beneficiaries away from alternative supplemental coverage (such as private employer-sponsored benefits) that generally require premiums, include some cost-sharing, and often also include other aspects of managed care (particularly with preferred-provider networks). These features of TFL are likely to increase beneficiaries' health care use[2] and alone might motivate DoD—and Medicare—to seek opportunities to encourage beneficiaries to use services efficiently.

However, there is little room for utilization management under standard Medicare as it is currently structured, and thus there is no room for such management under TFL. Given the statutory limitations to requiring care or utilization management under standard Medicare, the main option available to DoD for implementing managed care strategies for TFL beneficiaries is to induce them to accept such management voluntarily.

The most plausible mechanism for doing so is via an MTF. About 10 percent of military beneficiaries age 65 or older used MTFs for all or most of their care prior to implementation of the TFL program. While some beneficiaries may have been drawn to an MTF primarily to save on medical expenses, many prefer the military health care system and, given a choice, would use MTFs over civilian providers even if there were no financial advantages

---

[1] The term "managed care" is used in the literature in many different ways to refer to methods as diverse as the use of preferred provider networks, primary care gatekeeping, preauthorization requirements, and utilization review. However, the usual meaning, and the one that applies here, is health plans with organizational features that are intended to encourage the efficient use of health care.

[2] The lack of utilization management is a concern for Medicare generally and, among other factors, led to the development of the Medicare+Choice (now the Medicare Select) HMO program. However, enrollment in Medicare Select plans is voluntary (formerly on a monthly basis, but now on an annual basis). Perhaps more important, the availability and relative appeal of these plans has been declining.

in doing so. The Health Care Survey of DoD Beneficiaries[3] conducted shortly after TFL was enacted found that 90 percent of those using MTFs for all or most of their care wanted to continue the same level of use in the future. When beneficiaries who were using MTFs for only some or no care but wanted to use MTFs more extensively in the future are also taken into account, 39 percent of all TFL beneficiaries preferred to use MTFs for all or most of their care (TRICARE Management Activity, 2001b).[4]

The remainder of this chapter reviews options for managing MTF care for Medicare-eligible beneficiaries, with particular focus on DoD's new TRICARE Plus program.

TRICARE Plus and the MacDill-65 Demonstration

In passing the FY2001 NDAA, Congress encouraged DoD to implement "primary care empanelment" programs patterned on the MacDill-65 demonstration, which was conducted from September 1998 through September 2001 at MacDill Air Force Base in Tampa, Florida. This led to the development of TRICARE Plus, which gives some TFL beneficiaries access to primary care from MTF providers with the same priority as they would have for access to primary care as TRICARE Prime enrollees.

The MacDill-65 demonstration had several goals:

- It was intended to improve access to MTF care for some Medicare-eligible military retirees who desired MTF care, without increasing MTF capacity.[5] Under MacDill-65, MTF resources were increased by $2 million per year. However, the long-term expectation was that empanelment would concentrate primary care MTF services among a smaller number of beneficiaries than had previously been served under the space-available access policy, but with no overall increase in an MTF's level of effort.
- It was intended to preserve existing clinical relationships with MTF primary care providers (PCPs), e.g., for former TRICARE Senior Prime and MacDill-65 enrollees and for TRICARE Prime beneficiaries who turn 65.
- It was intended to further the achievement of DoD's benefits mission by improving quality of care and beneficiary satisfaction while lowering costs, relative to what beneficiaries would have experienced under the MTF space-available policy and standard Medicare prior to TFL.
- It was intended to further the achievement of DoD's readiness mission by creating a flexible and cost-effective source of referrals to MTF specialists.

TRICARE Plus was established with similar goals. MacDill-65 had the additional goal of using pharmacy management to improve quality of care and to lower costs; to our knowledge, TRICARE Plus does not automatically include pharmacy management.

---

[3] Available at http://www.tricare.osd.mil/survey/hcsurvey/default.htm.

[4] In interviews conducted for this project, TMA staff and representatives from retiree organizations expected that many Medicare-eligible military retirees would prefer to receive care at MTFs than from civilian providers and that many such beneficiaries might be disappointed by TFL because it does not guarantee them access to MTFs.

[5] Air Force personnel with whom we spoke referred to the goal of providing "meaningful" access to MTF care, by which they meant access that facilitated ongoing patient relationships with particular providers, and continuity of care; they characterized the prior space-available policy as fostering neither.

Under MacDill-65, a limited number of Medicare-eligible military retirees living in the MacDill catchment area were entitled to receive primary care from MTF providers with the same priority for access to primary care as TRICARE Prime beneficiaries have. The intent was for each enrollee to establish a clinical relationship with a particular PCP. The PCP would also coordinate any specialty care that the patient may need, facilitating referrals to MTF or community providers as appropriate. MTF staff would coordinate pharmacy use for enrollees. Given the statutory prohibition against Medicare reimbursement for MTF care, DoD covered the cost of all services provided at the MTF. However, care provided in the community was paid under Medicare, even if the referral had been made by an MTF PCP. Enrollees were not locked out of seeking care in the community on their own (i.e., under Medicare), but they were encouraged to allow their PCP to coordinate their care.

Eligible beneficiaries were invited to apply to MacDill-65, and approximately 2,000 beneficiaries were randomly selected from those who applied. Patients' clinical characteristics had no effect on their chances of being offered enrollment in the demonstration.[6]

DoD developed TRICARE Plus after the passage of the FY 2001 NDAA. For Medicare-eligible military retirees, its overall design is very similar to MacDill-65.[7] TRICARE Plus includes several changes, largely to make it a national program:

- All MTFs are eligible to offer TRICARE Plus. Each MTF commander determines whether his or her MTF participates and the number of beneficiaries who can enroll. TRICARE Plus is not intended to lead to expansion in MTF capacity.
- TRICARE Plus enrollment is not portable across MTFs (but beneficiaries remain eligible for care on a space-available basis at other MTFs).
- Beneficiaries who are currently enrolled in an HMO or similar program are precluded from enrolling in TRICARE Plus under the assumption that they have existing relationships with providers outside the MTF.
- The highest priority for TRICARE Plus enrollment is given to eligible beneficiaries who had previously been enrolled in TRICARE Senior Prime or MacDill-65. The next-highest priority is given to eligible beneficiaries who have clinical characteristics such that their participation would further an MTF's readiness mission. Beneficiaries who turn 65 and who have previously been enrolled in TRICARE Prime have third priority.
- Enrollees who do not comply with the recommendations of their MTF PCP are to be counseled to disenroll from the program.

---

[6] There was one exception: A small number of very sick patients were asked to forgo enrollment because they predominantly used specialty care and were thus thought to derive relatively little benefit from a primary care demonstration program.

[7] TRICARE Plus is also available to the dependents of active duty personnel who are not enrolled in TRICARE Prime and to military retirees and their dependents under age 65. Except as noted, however, we focus on TRICARE Plus as it pertains to Medicare-eligible military retirees.

Goals and Assumptions for the TRICARE Plus Program

To our knowledge, MacDill-65 has not been formally evaluated, and such evaluation is outside the scope of this report. In this section, however, we examine the assumptions underlying the main goals for the TRICARE Plus program.

Improve MTF Access

Relative to the space-available policy, some TFL beneficiaries should have improved access to MTFs under TRICARE Plus. For instance, no beneficiary is assured of receiving space-available care, but TRICARE Plus enrollees are guaranteed access to MTF primary care and continue to have access to MTF specialty care on a space-available basis. In addition, because TRICARE Plus is designed to foster relationships between beneficiaries and specific PCPs and to ensure consistent access, it may improve access to MTFs for enrolled beneficiaries relative to the space-available policy.

Whether TRICARE Plus succeeds in meeting the goal of improving MTF access will depend on a number of factors: the number and distribution of available TRICARE Plus openings relative to the level and distribution of demand for MTF access by Medicare-eligible military retirees; whether TRICARE Plus's access standards are met; and the effect of TRICARE Plus on space-available specialty care for TFL beneficiaries.[8]

Preserve Existing Clinical Relationships

TRICARE Plus is explicitly designed to preserve existing clinical relationships by giving beneficiaries who have an existing primary care relationship with a military provider at their local MTF the highest priority for enrollment (and precluding enrollment for beneficiaries who have current primary care relationships via a non-military HMO). In contrast, the space-available policy does not guarantee any TFL beneficiaries access to MTF primary care, let alone to a particular PCP.

However, in practice, continuity in the relationship with a specific provider requires that the provider remain available to a given patient. This may be difficult to ensure if primary care is mainly provided by military personnel because such personnel frequently move from one posting to another (during deployments and in other situations). Provider continuity could be enhanced by using civilian PCPs in MTFs, assuming they could be recruited efficiently, but this would presumably limit whatever benefits the TRICARE Plus program might provide for DoD's readiness mission. Also, beneficiaries may gain from continuity of access to the same treatment facility even if the individual clinicians change—for instance, if medical records are easier to maintain or if the handoff between providers is better within facilities than across them.

Improve Quality of Care and Beneficiary Satisfaction and Lower Costs

This goal seems most directly related to DoD's benefits mission. In many ways, the promise of managed care is to control costs while maintaining or improving quality of care. As discussed above, the combination of Medicare and TFL includes few of the mechanisms that

---

[8] TRICARE Plus is designed to have no negative effects on access to MTF care for TRICARE Prime enrollees, but there is the empirical question of whether this holds in practice. As the TMA has stated in TRICARE Plus policy memos, any such reduction in MTF access would be likely to increase DoD's costs because DoD would be required to pay for care provided to TRICARE Prime enrollees by community providers, via managed care support contractors.

other plans use to manage care, such as preferred-provider networks, preauthorization requirements, utilization review, or care management and coordination.

TRICARE Plus may present an opportunity to implement some of these mechanisms, although it is not designed to use all of them. In particular, PCPs under TRICARE Plus come from a preferred provider network: MTF providers. Similarly, while enrollees can choose to receive specialty care from any provider (and may not have access to MTF specialty providers), PCPs are likely to have some influence over this choice.

TRICARE Plus may present an opportunity to introduce some degree of care management by taking advantage of beneficiaries' desire for MTF care, i.e., by making it a de facto condition of participation that enrollees comply with the recommendations of their PCP.[9] Numerous studies have shown the benefits of care management and well-planned systems for using nurse or PCP case managers to improve outcomes for particular chronic conditions, including diabetes,[10] congestive heart failure,[11] asthma,[12] and depression.[13] At the same time, there is evidence that care management is relatively less effective among a population of generally high-risk patients (i.e., patients with a range of conditions who are predicted to have high medical costs) than a targeted group of patients with a particular condition (Boult et al., 2000a). Also, there is little evidence regarding the clinical benefits or cost-effectiveness of care management in a general population.

These results suggest that TRICARE Plus could have clinical benefits for patients with certain medical conditions if targeted and implemented in particular ways. However, our understanding is that there are no specific plans to target TRICARE Plus enrollment to patients with particular conditions, e.g., those for which there is evidence of clinical benefits from care management.[14] Nor do we know of any plans to introduce evidence-based care management practices as part of TRICARE Plus. The lack of such plans seems likely to limit the opportunities to improve patients' outcomes via primary care management.

Furthermore, there is relatively little evidence that care management reduces total health care costs. While some cases of care management having reduced health care costs have been documented in the literature, it appears that in other cases—and perhaps more commonly—care management programs increase total health care costs.[15] As a result, it cannot be assumed that TRICARE Plus will necessarily reduce the overall cost to the federal government of providing health care to program enrollees.

Finally, there is the question of the cost of providing particular health care services in MTFs relative to the private sector. In principle, even if MTFs are less efficient than civilian

---

[9] This may be hard to implement in practice. However, staff responsible for MacDill-65 indicated that, in extreme cases of patient non-compliance, staff recommended to patients that they discontinue the program.

[10] See, for example, Aubert et al., 1998; Renders et al., 2001.

[11] See, for example, Heidenreich, Ruggerio, and Massie, 1999; Philbin, 1999; Rich, 1999.

[12] See, for example, Gemignani, 1998.

[13] See, for example, Wells et al., 2000; Schoenbaum et al., 2001.

[14] In our interviews with DoD personnel, they mentioned the possibility that such targeting could constitute discrimination, unless it were specifically intended to further DoD's readiness mission; as discussed above, TRICARE Plus provides for giving higher priority to certain beneficiaries in such cases.

[15] Relatively few studies report cost-effectiveness of particular interventions from the perspective of the provider system or the health plan. More commonly, cost studies report implementation cost but do not report, let alone monetize, the benefits to the delivery organization, whereas cost-effectiveness studies report results from a societal perspective (e.g., Gold et al., 1996), which may differ substantially from the perspective of the delivery organization.

providers in providing care, primary care management that reduces the total amount of health care use could reduce direct treatment costs relative to unmanaged Medicare plus TFL. However, savings are obviously more likely if MTFs are relatively efficient providers of care. Further research is needed to address the efficiency of MTF care relative to the civilian sector.

In sum, in the particular context of TFL and TRICARE Plus, it seems unlikely that the savings (if any) of care management will offset the costs DoD incurs in providing this benefit. This is because DoD bears the full cost of primary care management (and other care) provided at MTFs but only the Medicare cost-sharing amount for care provided in the community. In that sense, it is almost certainly less costly for DoD to reduce the amount of MTF services provided to TFL beneficiaries, at least in the absence of payment by Medicare for care provided in MTFs. The subject of Medicare payment for care in MTFs is discussed further in Chapter Five.

Meet DoD's Readiness Mission

DoD staff consistently indicated that DoD's ability to meet its readiness mission depends on a continued flow of elderly patients to MTFs. Several reasons were cited:

- To ensure that providers are satisfied with their case mix (e.g., because elderly patients are more likely to have conditions that providers find challenging to treat)
- To meet the requirements of DoD's graduate medical and continuing medical education programs (e.g., because training programs require a certain case mix of patients)
- To ensure preparedness for deployments (because providers' readiness requires them to diagnose and treat patients with complex conditions on an ongoing basis, and elderly patients are more likely to have such conditions).

Thus, there appeared to be a widespread perception within DoD that treating elderly patients at MTFs would be cost-effective for the federal government for two reasons.[16] The first reason is that DoD's medical education programs would not be feasible without those patients.[17] The second is that the clinical capacity at MTFs that is required to meet DoD's readiness mission would be underutilized, or incorrectly utilized, if MTF providers did not treat elderly patients. In this sense, the true marginal cost of treating elderly patients is perceived within DoD as being relatively low, independent of whether care management reduces direct treatment costs. In our view, these arguments are plausible under certain conditions, which may or may not apply in practice.

It seems plausible that MTF providers would prefer the more continuous relationships with patients afforded by TRICARE Plus to practice patterns under the space-available policy, furthering the goal of provider satisfaction. On the other hand, it is unclear whether the case mix of TRICARE Plus enrollees will facilitate provider readiness. TRICARE Plus

---

[16] We note that such patients need not be limited to military retirees. Indeed, DoD personnel expressed the view that DoD and Medicare would benefit if MTF providers could treat the general Medicare population (with at least partial reimbursement from Medicare).

[17] The significance of this obviously depends on whether or how DoD's medical education programs contribute to the achievement of DoD's readiness (or benefits) missions. These issues were outside the scope of this report but may warrant separate examination.

implementation guidelines appear to permit giving eligible beneficiaries with certain clinical conditions high or even highest priority for program enrollment, and we understand that the TMA has directed MTF commanders to consider these factors in implementing TRICARE Plus. But such targeted enrollment may be difficult to implement in practice if, for instance, commanders face pressure from beneficiaries for "equitable" access without regard to clinical status, or if they lack the data necessary to target case mix.[18, 19]

In addition, primary care management per se may not necessarily further the readiness mission. In particular, it is unclear whether treating the types of patients that have been shown to benefit from primary care management (i.e., those with chronic conditions such as diabetes, congestive heart failure, or asthma) helps providers prepare for battlefield medicine, which emphasizes acute trauma care, diagnosis and treatment of acute disease, and nonbattle injury.

In practice, there is likely to be variation across MTFs in the effects of TRICARE Plus on training and readiness. For instance, the impact of serving a greater number of Medicare-eligible beneficiaries (or a different patient mix than under the space-available policy) may be limited at many MTFs but relatively more important at referral centers where PCPs can refer TRICARE Plus patients to medical subspecialists. The TRICARE Plus implementation guidelines permit the program to be implemented differently at different locations; therefore, in principle, it may be possible to focus the program on MTFs where it is most likely to further DoD's readiness mission.

Conclusions and Recommendations

In sum, relatively little opportunity exists to implement managed care practices under standard Medicare and TFL. However, given the apparent desire of many TFL beneficiaries to receive care from military providers, DoD may have the opportunity to manage care for some elderly beneficiaries via programs instituted at MTFs. Currently, this requires DoD to assume full responsibility for the cost of care provided to Medicare-eligible beneficiaries at MTFs.

We find it likely that TRICARE Plus and similar programs will be well received by beneficiaries, especially since participation is voluntary. We also find it plausible that such programs could improve clinical outcomes for some enrollees, relative to both standard Medicare and the current space-available policy. However, the scope of such improvements depends critically on how and for whom care management programs are implemented.

As currently conceived, TRICARE Plus would function primarily as a mechanism to ensure that some elderly patients continue to use MTFs as their source of care, rather than using their Medicare and TFL benefits in the community. It seems plausible that care management through MTF providers could improve outcomes and/or reduce total health care costs for some patients, relative to unmanaged care under Medicare or the space-available

---

[18] Under MacDill-65, for instance, eligibility and enrollment were largely independent of patients' clinical status; the exception was patients with particularly complex needs, who were intentionally excluded from participation because of the expectation that they would not benefit from primary care management.

[19] Technically, the relevant case mix is that of the overall MTF patient population, including those with TRICARE Prime. Thus, TRICARE Plus beneficiaries should be used to fill in gaps in the desired MTF case mix.

policy. DoD may be able to increase the likelihood of such benefits by targeting TRICARE Plus enrollment to patients who are likely to benefit from primary care management and implementing effective care management programs for these patients.

However, since Medicare is currently prohibited by statute from paying for care in MTFs, DoD must assume full responsibility for the cost of care provided to Medicare-eligible beneficiaries at MTFs. As a result, DoD's patient care costs are almost certainly higher under TRICARE Plus than if care were provided under Medicare. On the other hand, treating Medicare-eligible beneficiaries in MTFs helps DoD fulfill its readiness mission. How these factors balance on net is unknown, and further research regarding the effects of MTF primary care management on patient outcomes and treatment costs, and regarding providers' case-mix preferences and the relationship between primary care management and readiness is necessary to determine the overall cost-effectiveness of TRICARE Plus from the perspective of DoD and the federal government, relative to alternative models for care management and readiness training. In the next chapter, we discuss potential models for Medicare sharing in the costs of MTF care.

CHAPTER FIVE

Models for Medicare's Sharing in Military Treatment Facility Costs

Currently, the Medicare program has no financial liability for MTF services (other than emergency services) provided to TFL beneficiaries.[1] A statutory prohibition on payments to federal providers, part of the original Medicare law, was intended to prevent shifting costs to Medicare for care already being provided under federal programs such as the Indian Health Service (IHS), Department of Veterans Affairs (DVA), and DoD. Over the years, statutory changes have been made to allow payment for services provided by the IHS, but the prohibition on Medicare payment for care in DoD and VA facilities remains.

Prior to TFL, the responsibility for Medicare military retirees was determined by where the care was furnished: Medicare was solely responsible for civilian care (for Medicare-covered benefits), and DoD assumed all costs for space-available care provided by MTFs to Medicare beneficiaries. In FY2000, DoD spent an estimated $1.4 billion on direct care for dual eligibles (Department of Defense, 2002). Under TFL, DoD now has responsibility as the secondary payer for civilian care but continues to have sole responsibility for direct care. DoD was expected to spend an estimated $3.9 billion in FY2002 on secondary payments for civilian care furnished to Medicare beneficiaries (Department of Defense, 2002).

DoD's new obligations for TFL beneficiaries raise issues related to the cost of furnishing direct care relative to making secondary payments for civilian care and elevates the issue of whether Medicare should share in the costs of direct care services now that the traditional division of responsibilities for military retiree health care costs no longer exists. If Medicare is to share in direct care costs, a further issue is whether it should participate as primary payer or on some other basis that continues to assign primary responsibility for the direct care furnished to TFL beneficiaries to DoD.

Without Medicare cost-sharing for MTF care, DoD's costs would be lower if TFL beneficiaries who are currently receiving MTF direct care would instead obtain care from civilian providers; however, the shift could negatively affect physician retention and training, create excess capacity at some MTFs, and would be counter to the preferences of many TFL beneficiaries. Moreover, Medicare costs would increase substantially because the program would become primary payer for civilian care that had previously been furnished by MTFs at no cost to Medicare. Only about 41 percent of beneficiaries residing within MTF catchment areas use civilian care exclusively (Levy and Miller, 1998), and the Medicare per capita sav-

---

[1] Section 1814(c) of the Social Security Act. Exceptions are made if (1) the provider is furnishing services to the public generally as a community institution or agency, (2) emergency hospital services are involved, or (3) services were furnished by a Department of Veterans Affairs (DVA) hospital in good faith to an individual who is subsequently determined to not be entitled to VA health benefits.

ings attributable to MTF use is substantial.[2] Thus, Medicare has an interest in assuring that direct care for TFL beneficiaries continues.

The pre-TFL division of responsibilities between TRICARE and Medicare resulted in each program viewing dual eligible beneficiaries independently. Medicare cost-sharing for MTF care would foster viewing TFL beneficiaries as a joint responsibility and lead to finding ways to provide them with the highest-quality care at the least cost to the federal government. It would provide DoD with financial resources to continue to provide direct care to TFL beneficiaries and has the potential to meet several policy goals: allow TFL beneficiaries the choice between direct and civilian care, serve DoD's readiness needs, and most important, provide high-quality health care services to TFL beneficiaries and the non-retiree military population at the least cost to the federal government.

This chapter explores potential models for Medicare's sharing in the costs of direct care services provided to TFL beneficiaries that could potentially reduce overall federal health care costs. We first provide a conceptual policy framework for Medicare cost-sharing and evaluation of alternative cost-sharing models. We discuss the financial incentives under TFL and the cost implications if beneficiaries shift from MTF to civilian care. We also describe the "lessons learned" from a Medicare-DoD subvention demonstration that have applicability to cost-sharing arrangements. Next, we discuss three potential models for Medicare's sharing in the costs of direct care services provided to TFL fee-for-service beneficiaries through payments to the TFL accrual fund. Any of the models would require statutory changes to implement on any basis other than a demonstration basis. Next, we discuss payments for MTF care furnished to Medicare+Choice enrollees. The chapter ends with conclusions and recommendations.

Policy Framework for Medicare Cost-Sharing

DoD and CMS share the common goals of providing TFL beneficiaries with

- high-quality, cost-effective care and
- choice in where that care is obtained.

Both programs also have the goal of minimizing the costs to their respective programs for TFL beneficiaries. DoD has additional goals that are not shared by Medicare:

- To provide high-quality, cost-effective care for non-TFL beneficiaries
- To maintain readiness to provide medical care in case of deployments or war
- To fulfill the social contract with TFL beneficiaries without limiting MTF access for other TRICARE enrollees.

With the implementation of the TFL program, direct care services play a somewhat less critical role in fulfilling DoD's social contract with its retirees because TFL beneficiaries now have access to civilian care at no cost. DoD's secondary payments for civilian care allevi-

---

[2] The U.S. General Accounting Office (GAO) estimated that largely because of MTF usage, Medicare's fee-for-service payments for Senior Prime enrollees in the absence of the DoD-Medicare subvention demonstration would have been on average 55 percent of the Senior Prime rate (U.S. General Accounting Office, 2001c).

ates some pressure to make direct care available to TFL beneficiaries and, as a result, DoD's budgetary constraints, access for non-TFL beneficiaries, and readiness considerations assume increased importance in decisions regarding the extent to which direct care services should be made available to TFL beneficiaries.

From an overall policy perspective, the public interest will be best served if DoD and Medicare view TFL beneficiaries as a joint responsibility and work toward a cost-sharing arrangement that meets the following objectives:

- High-quality care at the lowest overall cost
- Beneficiary choice between using an MTF or civilian providers
- Flexibility for DoD in determining MTF service levels for TFL beneficiaries, taking into account readiness considerations and access for non-TFL beneficiaries.

We believe that it will be in the national public interest to focus on these objectives rather than trying to decide whether it is "equitable" for Medicare to become the primary payer for MTF care provided to TFL beneficiaries. The equity argument that is commonly advanced contends that DoD and military personnel pay Medicare employer and employee taxes but, to the extent that MTFs are utilized, they do not receive the full insurance benefits to which they are entitled. From Medicare's perspective, TFL beneficiaries are entitled to the full Medicare benefit package but elect not to utilize certain benefits just as other beneficiary groups (e.g., those living overseas) do. At any time, they may exercise their right to receive the full Medicare benefit package by going to civilian providers.

Unlike the IHS, whose sole mission is to provide health benefits, the military health system has both a benefit and a readiness function and DoD has the discretion to eliminate direct care for TFL beneficiaries whenever it is no longer in DoD's interests to provide the services. The equity argument is predicated on a premise that MTFs should be treated the same as any other provider of services to Medicare beneficiaries. Yet, unlike Medicare providers who are not allowed to have discriminatory admission policies for Medicare patients, MTFs need to be able to discriminate between TFL beneficiaries and other military beneficiaries and among TFL beneficiaries in order to meet readiness objectives and the needs of non-TFL military beneficiaries.

Cost Implications of Direct and Civilian Care: A Conceptual Model

As seen in Table 5.1, the site where TFL beneficiaries receive medical care has significant financial implications for both DoD and Medicare. The CMS goal to protect Medicare trust funds and minimize its costs is best served if beneficiaries obtain care from MTF providers. The financial implications for DoD are more complicated because space-available capacity affects not only the costs of providing MTF care to TFL beneficiaries but also health care access and costs for other DoD beneficiaries. In addition, the value of meeting readiness objectives and fulfilling the social contract with military retirees needs to be weighed against the cost considerations. Generally, however, DoD's costs are minimized if Medicare-covered care is received outside the MTFs.

Table 5.1
Comparison of Direct Care and Civilian Service Providers' Fee-for-Service Liabilities for Medicare-Covered Services Under TFL

Service Provider	Medicare Liability	TRICARE Liability	Supplemental Insurance Liability	Beneficiary Liability
Military Treatment Facility	None	Cost of care, net of any supplemental insurance	Amount that would have been payable if beneficiary had received a Medicare-covered service: Part A and Part B deductibles, preventative services, and drugs	None for outpatient care; minimal subsistence charges for inpatient stays ($11 per diem)
Civilian	Medicare payment rate less applicable deductible and coinsurance amounts	Pays beneficiary's deductible, coinsurance, and balanced billing amounts (unless covered by supplemental insurance)	Coinsurance, deductible, and balanced billing amounts to the extent covered by policy	None

As discussed in Chapter Three, TFL beneficiaries face no out-of-pocket costs if they obtain care from a civilian provider. Those with supplemental insurance have a strong incentive to drop their policies because they are no longer cost-effective given the new pharmacy benefit and TRICARE supplemental coverage. While TFL beneficiaries no longer have a financial incentive to use the MTF, many prefer the military health system.

Table 5.2 summarizes the effect that beneficiaries switching from MTF to civilian care would have on DoD's costs, Medicare's costs, and total federal government costs. Given beneficiary preferences for MTF care, this switch is likely to occur only if DoD reduces its MTF service level for TFL beneficiaries. If the MTF is operating at or over capacity, there should be little impact on MTF costs assuming that non-Medicare patients fill the appointments no longer used by Medicare patients. The impact on TRICARE costs for non-Medicare patients depends on how direct care costs compare with payments that would have been made to civilian providers, and the services would have been forgone with longer MTF waiting times. The secondary payments for Medicare-covered civilian care furnished to TFL beneficiaries would increase DoD's costs. In addition, there could be implications for physician retention and readiness because patient mix would not be as rich.

Medicare's costs would increase not only as the primary payer for the civilian-provided services but also because of the probable increases in demand resulting from the lack of beneficiary cost-sharing (see Chapter Three). The shift would be largely between Medicare and DoD with limited impact on the overall federal budget. Because TRICARE follows the Medicare payment methodologies, payment rates for civilian providers should be fairly comparable for the Medicare and non-Medicare population and have minimal effect on total federal outlays. Overall, higher expenditures would result from increased demand (from both the Medicare and non-Medicare populations) and TRICARE secondary payments (which would not have been made for non-Medicare patients obtaining civilian care). If an MTF is operating below capacity, the increase in total federal outlays would be greater, assuming that the combined Medicare-DoD payments for civilian care would be higher than the incremental costs of MTF care (see the discussion in the subsection that follows).

Table 5.2
Impact of Beneficiaries Switching from MTF Direct Care to Civilian Care

Impact on DoD	Impact on Medicare	Net Impact on Federal Budget
Reduces MTF space-available demand; impact depends on MTF capacity. MTF at or over capacity: • Improves waiting times for non-Medicare population • Little effect on total MTF costs (except to extent it avoids need to expand capacity) • Costs increase for coinsurance/deductibles for Medicare population • Cost impact for non-Medicare population depends on costs of MTF care relative to civilian care payments (with some increase for services that would have been forgone) • Some impact on readiness to the extent the younger population does not present conditions as complex. MTF below capacity: • MTF has variable cost savings but fixed costs spread over fewer patients. • Secondary payer costs increase for civilian care furnished to TFL beneficiaries. • Having fewer patients reduces readiness capabilities.	Shift in services from MTF to civilian providers increases program costs. Full coverage eliminates beneficiary incentives to control utilization of civilian providers and increases program costs.	Depends on MTF capacity. MTF at or above capacity: • Costs increase because of DoD secondary payments and increased beneficiary demand. MTF below capacity: • Costs increase assuming MTF can provide care at less cost than the cost of payments to a civilian provider.

In summary, if DoD reduces MTF service levels for TFL beneficiaries, total federal outlays are likely to increase regardless of whether the MTF is operating at or below capacity. A cost-sharing arrangement that encourages efficient and coordinated care and reduces total federal outlays would serve the public interest. Medicare has the most to lose financially if a substantial number of beneficiaries switch from MTF to civilian care (and the most to gain if Medicare beneficiaries switch from civilian to MTF care). As long as CMS has safeguards to assure that Medicare's total financial liabilities (price and volume) would be lower than its liabilities in the absence of an arrangement, a cost-sharing agreement would be consistent with its goals. DoD's underlying interest is whether Medicare's payments would be sufficient to cover the marginal costs of providing MTF care relative to being the secondary payer under Medicare and whether there would be sufficient flexibility to respond to changes in readiness and in the service delivery needs of non-TFL patients.

Comparative Costs of Direct and Civilian Care

The assumption that total payments for civilian care would exceed the incremental cost of MTF care provided to TFL beneficiaries is one that merits further investigation. Cost comparisons for individual services are difficult to make because MTF costs for outpatient services are aggregated at the visit level. Detailed data on the individual services provided during an outpatient visit and on incremental costs are not readily available.[3] The more im-

---

[3] With the phase-in of itemized billing that began in FY2002, the comparisons should be easier to make in the future. Itemized billing information is needed, for example, to compare the amounts that would be payable on a fee-for-service

portant question, however, is not how costs compare on a service-by-service basis but how they would compare in the aggregate taking utilization and health status into account.

Studies have consistently found that the military population utilizes more services than the civilian population and that utilization rates are higher for direct care than civilian care. Frequently cited causes for the higher utilization rates are minimal copayments for civilian care and free direct care and, with regard to direct care, fewer incentives historically for efficient practice styles and lower ratios of support staff to health care providers (Hosek et al., 1995; Klerman and Kilburn, 1998; U.S. General Accounting Office, 2002). However, it is not entirely clear the extent to which the higher utilization rates are primarily a characteristic of the military population, or a provider characteristic (i.e., military providers have a more resource-intensive practice style than their civilian counterparts), or a combination of the two.

The question of the comparative costs of direct and civilian care is slightly different in the context of a cost-sharing agreement for TFL beneficiaries designed to reduce overall federal spending than it was in earlier utilization studies; namely, the question is whether (in the absence of copayments for care obtained in either venue (MTF or civilian) the combined Medicare-DoD payments for civilian care exceed the *incremental* costs of providing MTF care. This issue has implications for a Medicare cost-sharing model:

- If the higher utilization pattern is largely a population characteristic, the assumption that the costs of civilian care will exceed the incremental costs of MTF care is stronger, and there is more support for adopting a cost-sharing model as a means of reducing overall federal costs.
- If the higher utilization pattern is largely a provider characteristic, there is less certainty that the incremental costs of MTF care would be lower and less support for an argument that a cost-sharing agreement would be in the public interest. At a minimum, a cost-sharing agreement that protects the Medicare program from paying more in the aggregate for direct care than it would for civilian care would be needed to assure total federal outlays do not increase.

From the perspective of total federal outlays, it would be desirable to have a better understanding of how utilization by TFL beneficiaries who obtain care primarily from MTFs compares with that of TFL beneficiaries who obtain care solely through civilian providers before the adoption of Medicare cost-sharing policies that would encourage an expansion of MTF care for TFL beneficiaries.

Lessons Learned from the DoD-Medicare Subvention Demonstration

The Balanced Budget Act of 1997 required that DoD and Medicare implement a subvention demonstration to test the feasibility of making Medicare-covered services available to Medicare-eligible DoD beneficiaries age 65 or older through the TRICARE program and MTFs, which would then be eligible for payments from Medicare. The statute provided for two distinct models: TRICARE Senior Prime and Medicare Partners. TRICARE Senior Prime was

---

basis for MTF outpatient care using the Medicare payment schedules with the amounts that would be payable using DoD reimbursement rates that apply to other payers.

implemented at six demonstration sites and ended December 31, 2001. Medicare Partners has not been implemented.

Under the TRICARE Senior Prime model, the demonstration sites operated managed-care plans meeting the certification requirements for Medicare+Choice organizations. Medicare beneficiaries who enrolled in Senior Prime chose a military care manager at a participating MTF. They received their primary care from the MTF. Other services were provided either by the MTF or by civilian providers in the Senior Prime network.

The capitation payment rates for Senior Prime were negotiated by DoD and the Health Care Financing Administration (HCFA, the predecessor agency to CMS). Medicare paid for Senior Prime enrollees' care only after DoD met a level-of-effort threshold, that is, DoD spent as much for health care services for Medicare beneficiaries (both enrollees and nonenrollees) as it had in the past across the six sites. The criteria for meeting the level-of-effort threshold were complicated and difficult to understand.[4] The complexity made the final payment determination, which was made retroactively, difficult to predict. As a result, MTFs incurred costs for Senior Prime enrollees within a fixed budget without knowing whether they would be reimbursed. In fact, DoD did not retain any first-year Medicare payments. Other issues raised by the demonstration include the adequacy of the capitation rate, the timeliness of the data used to establish the level-of-effort threshold, and the failure to align financial incentives to manage use of civilian care and encourage cost-effective service delivery (Farley et al., 2000, 2003; U.S. General Accounting Office, 2001c, 2001d, and 2002). The U.S. General Accounting Office (GAO) estimates that compared with similar Medicare fee-for-service beneficiaries, Senior Prime enrollees were hospitalized 41 percent more often and had 58 percent more outpatient visits (U.S. General Accounting Office, 2001c).

Some of the lessons learned from TRICARE Senior Prime have applicability to designing a mechanism for Medicare to share in the cost of MTF services furnished to TFL beneficiaries on either a fee-for-service or partial-capitation basis:

- The funding policies should be simple to understand so that management decisions can support an appropriate balance of MTF and civilian care for TFL beneficiaries. DoD managers should be able to predict the net costs of providing MTF care to TFL beneficiaries and weigh those costs with access and cost considerations for other DoD beneficiaries and readiness needs.
- Ideally, funding for TFL beneficiaries at the MTF level should be prospectively determined. Because MTFs operate within a fixed budget, MTF commanders should know in advance how much they would receive for furnishing services to TFL beneficiaries. If the cost-sharing arrangement incorporates a level-of-effort concept, any adjustments to account for level of effort should be handled as a separate budget transaction and not affect payments to individual MTFs.
- Financial incentives should be created at the MTF level that encourage efficient delivery of services. Bundled payments, such as ambulatory payment groups for outpatient care and diagnosis-related groups for inpatient care, create more incentives for efficiency relative to fee-for-service payments for individual services but do not dis-

---

[4] The level-of-effort calculation is controversial and DoD feels strongly that the amounts calculated for Senior Prime were not an accurate representation of the true level of effort.

courage unnecessary admissions or outpatient visits. Full or partial capitation provides more incentives for cost-effective practice patterns than a bundled payment for each encounter.

- In a fee-for-service cost-sharing arrangement, the Medicare payment rate for individual services should be fixed in advance with the recognition that utilization and total payments will vary across MTFs and time, based on space available and readiness considerations. In a partial-capitation arrangement, the MTF should pay for any services covered by the arrangement that are obtained from civilian providers.
- Care should be taken to provide incentives to encourage the appropriate weighing of readiness and access considerations for non-TFL beneficiaries in deciding service levels for TFL beneficiaries. To avoid crowding out non-TFL beneficiaries, funding for TFL beneficiaries should not be more generous.
- Attention should be given during the design of the cost-sharing arrangement to whether periodic adjustments should be made in the proportion of costs borne by Medicare and DoD based on more-recent data and the mechanism for making those adjustments.
- There are significant operational burdens associated with complying with Medicare requirements. While the Senior Prime burden was largely created by the Medicare+Choice requirements, Medicare requirements for fee-for-service payments entail not only itemized billings but also cost reporting requirements that may be difficult for DoD facilities to meet. Viewing MTF care for TFL beneficiaries as a joint responsibility of the Medicare and TRICARE programs instead of treating DoD the same as any other Medicare provider reduces the rationale for requiring compliance with burdensome Medicare rules.

Medicare Cost-Sharing for Fee-for-Service TFL Beneficiaries

Rationalizing the funding for direct care services for TFL beneficiaries can be best accomplished by separating the question of how funding to support direct care services to dual eligibles should be shared by DoD and Medicare from the question of appropriate payments to MTFs for these services.

The first question concerns the appropriate balance between Medicare and TRICARE funding for direct care that would best meet the needs of both programs and result in overall savings to the federal government. The accrual fund and the Medicare trust funds provide ready mechanisms for budget transfers between the two programs to implement the cost-sharing agreement once the policies are established. As mentioned earlier in this report, the FY2001 NDAA established an accrual fund to provide for mandatory funding for dual eligibles (including the under-65 Medicare/TRICARE beneficiaries). The fund recognizes DoD's accrued and future liability for the costs of MTF care, civilian care, and pharmacy benefits for dual-eligible retirees. Implemented in FY2003, the accrual funds will derive from annual treasury payments for the amortized actuarial unfunded accrued liability, from annual DoD contributions for the actuarial "normal cost" of the benefits, and from fund investment earnings. FY2003 fund outlays at the time of implementation were estimated to be $5.8 billion ($1.4 billion for MTF care and $4.4 billion for purchased care) (TRICARE Management Activity, 2002b).

The second question involves designing incentives at the MTF level that effectively promote the provision of cost-effective care to TFL beneficiaries, while also giving appropriate weight to readiness and access considerations. If Medicare payments were to flow to the accrual fund instead of directly to MTFs, DoD would have greater flexibility to design appropriate MTF-level incentives.

In the subsections that follow, we outline three basic policy options for Medicare's sharing in the costs of MTF care provided to TFL beneficiaries who are enrolled in the Medicare fee-for-service program.

- Model 1 would use a fee-for-service payment methodology for all dual eligibles receiving MTF care. That is, a Medicare payment would be made to the accrual fund for individual services furnished by MTFs for services to both under-65 and over-65 beneficiaries who are also entitled to Medicare benefits.
- Model 2 builds on TRICARE Plus and would apply to only the subset of TFL beneficiaries who choose to enroll in the program (see Chapter Four). Under this model, Medicare would make a partial-capitation payment for primary care services only for TRICARE Plus enrollees.
- Model 3 is a risk-sharing model under which Medicare would transfer to DoD any Medicare per capita savings for TRICARE Plus enrollees.

The models are designed to provide a conceptual framework for discussions on cost-sharing designs that would reduce overall federal costs and yet provide patients with better care. Further empirical work would be needed to analyze the potential cost implications of the options for DoD, Medicare, and total federal spending. While this analysis is needed to inform the discussion, it is likely the question of the appropriate balance between DoD and Medicare funding for MTF services provided to dual eligibles will undoubtedly be decided through the political process.

Model 1: Medicare Makes Fee-for-Service Payments for MTF Care

Under Model 1, Medicare would make fee-for-service payments based on itemized billings by MTFs for services furnished to all dual eligibles. Although MTFs would bill Medicare for the services, the Medicare payments would flow to the accrual fund. Medicare's payments could be based on either Medicare payment methodologies for services furnished by other providers or DoD's itemized billing rates (applicable to other third parties or to patients sponsored by other federal agencies).

If Medicare were the primary payer, DoD's contribution would be represented by the difference between Medicare's payment and the cost of providing MTF care. Depending on the relationship between Medicare payments and MTF costs, DoD's contribution could be either a cost or a source of revenue to DoD. In addition to shifting costs from DoD to Medicare, a fee-for-service cost-sharing arrangement that establishes Medicare as primary payer is likely to increase Medicare payments relative to the amounts that would be paid for civilian care for the following two reasons:

- Military facilities have higher utilization rates.
- For ambulatory services, civilian care in physician offices would be substituted for MTF outpatient clinic care, which generally has a higher Medicare payment because of the facility and physician components.

However, the concept that Medicare should be the primary payer does not recognize the social contract and readiness benefits that DoD derives from providing care to dual eligibles. Viewing the costs of direct care for dual eligibles as a joint responsibility would couple the Medicare fee-for-service payment discussed above with a DoD cost-sharing policy that goes beyond deductible and coinsurance amounts. It could, for example, be based on a level-of-effort concept that preserves the current relationship between DoD's and Medicare's expenditures for dual eligibles. Another cost-sharing policy would be for DoD to continue to pay for the fixed costs of MTF services furnished to dual eligibles. This would have the effect of limiting Medicare's payment to the estimated incremental costs of providing the services. The underlying policy rationale is that the TFL services are provided on a discretionary space-available basis. The incremental costs are the additional costs incurred by DoD in providing the services. In any event, negotiations would be required to establish an agreed-upon cost-sharing methodology that reflects the "lessons learned" from DoD-Medicare subvention demonstration.

If a cost-sharing arrangement were adopted, there are alternative ways to account for Medicare and DoD's respective contributions for the costs of direct care services furnished to dual eligibles:

- Medicare could withhold making payments to the accrual funds until the payments that would have otherwise been made were equivalent to the pre-determined level of DoD's contribution. This alternative would tie the withheld amounts to actual services provided on a fee-for-service basis. The incentive for DoD to provide MTF services to dual eligibles would not be strong because there would be no Medicare payment unless the level-of-effort requirement was met. Medicare payments for TFL beneficiaries would not be known until the end of the year. The model provides a strong financial incentive for MTF direct care only if a significant increase in overall usage over the base year is anticipated. This is most likely to occur at MTFs offering TRICARE Plus because Medicare fee-for-service beneficiaries will displace Medicare+ Choice enrollees.
- A withhold rate could be set prospectively, based on the expected level of MTF care in the payment year. Medicare's fee-for-service payments for MTF services throughout the year would be reduced by the prospectively determined offset rate, and there would be no reconciliation at the end of the year. The advantage of this alternative over the first alternative is that the Medicare payment amounts for direct care services furnished by MTFs would be established in advance.
- DoD could make a direct transfer of funds to the Medicare trust funds that would be equivalent to DoD's agreed-upon contribution. The transfer could be made (either annually or on a periodic basis) without regard to actual MTF usage by TFL beneficiaries. This alternative creates clearer incentives to provide direct care because no further adjustment would be made to Medicare payment levels. Because DoD's contribution has already been accounted for, DoD would have an incentive to furnish

direct care services to Medicare beneficiaries as long as the net costs of providing direct care (the incremental costs incurred by MTFs minus Medicare's fee-for-service payments) are less than DoD's secondary payer amounts for civilian care furnished to TFL beneficiaries.

Model 2: Medicare Pays Capitated Rate for Primary Care Services

Some state Medicaid programs use a primary care capitation model in which the provider is at risk for providing primary care services only. This approach could integrate well with the TRICARE Plus program (which currently involves only MTF primary care managers). Under the primary care capitation model, Medicare would make a capitated payment for TFL beneficiaries that enroll in TRICARE Plus. Payment would be based on current Medicare per capita expenditures for primary care services. In setting the rate, one issue would be the extent to which the higher utilization rates associated with military retirees should be reflected in the payment. Also, a negotiated reduction for DoD's contribution for the costs of care could be incorporated into the payment amount using either the "level-of-effort" or incremental cost approaches discussed for Model 1. An adjustment could be made for any Medicare payments for primary care services provided by civilian providers that would have been covered by the primary care capitation rate.

From DoD's viewpoint, this model is quite attractive because it capitalizes on the services that the MTFs are best equipped to provide without assuming responsibility and risk for specialty care. It would allow DoD to base its decisions on providing specialty care on readiness considerations. However, capitation for only primary care services creates an incentive to increase specialty care. (The lack of disincentives for referrals to the civilian network subvention may have been a factor in the high rates of specialty referrals in the subvention demonstration (Farley et al., 1999; U.S. General Accounting Office, 2002). DoD's continued responsibility for coinsurance amounts for civilian specialty care would help to counter incentives to substitute civilian specialty care for MTF primary and specialty direct care. However, the secondary payments may not provide a sufficient incentive at the MTF level as long as MTF and civilian care budgets are separate. Additional safeguards may need to be incorporated into the way the funds are allocated from the accrual fund to the MTFs to encourage the efficient utilization of specialty care.

Model 3: Medicare Shares Any Savings with DoD

Models 1 and 2 focus on Medicare sharing in the costs of MTF direct care services to Medicare beneficiaries. Model 3 takes a somewhat different approach by having Medicare share with DoD any savings that might accrue from MTF care provided to TFL beneficiaries. Potential Medicare savings would result from MTF direct care services for which Medicare would otherwise be the primary payer and, in the case of TRICARE Plus enrollees, MTF management of specialty care (MTF or civilian). The cost-savings arrangement could involve all TFL beneficiaries or be limited to TRICARE Plus enrollees. The savings would be the difference between Medicare's per capita expenditures for TFL (or only TRICARE Plus) beneficiaries and the average per capita expenditures for non-TFL beneficiaries. The comparison rates would be risk adjusted, and an issue would be whether further adjustments should be made for the higher utilization rates associated with military retirees.

Model 3 has several advantages over the two other models. It involves little administrative burden because there is no need to track MTF direct care services provided to TFL beneficiaries for purposes of Medicare cost-sharing. Second, there are incentives to manage both MTF direct care and civilian care for TRICARE Plus enrollees and to encourage provision of MTF direct care when it is more efficient to do so. Third, DoD is not at risk but has financial incentives to encourage cost-effective care. This model also includes flexibility to respond to changes in service needs and capacity. Fourth, this model does not put Medicare at risk for direct care services. DoD's and Medicare's share of any savings would be subject to negotiation.

Yet another variation would be to combine Models 2 and 3. Medicare would make a capitated payment for primary care services. Medicare would also share with DoD any savings attributable to nonprimary care services (after adjusting for any payments made on behalf of TRICARE Plus enrollees who use civilian primary care services).

Model 3 could also be used to share savings for coordinating care for TFL beneficiaries with complex chronic conditions. The Balanced Budget Act of 1997 authorized coordinated care demonstrations for supplemental routine care for chronically ill Medicare beneficiaries. CMS has selected 15 demonstration sites to test whether providing coordinated care services to Medicare beneficiaries with complex chronic conditions can lead to better patient outcomes without increasing program costs (*Medicare Fact Sheet,* 2001).

The coordinated care models collectively could serve as a model for a CMS/DoD demonstration involving a subset of dual eligibles who have one or more chronic illnesses and who require repeated hospitalizations. The opportunities for better outcomes and cost savings are greatest for this subset of beneficiaries. The TRICARE Plus enrollment process could include screening to identify these beneficiaries in addition to readiness-based screening. In the past, a major drawback to coordinated care demonstrations, particularly for the chronically ill or those with complex needs, has been the lack of Medicare drug coverage and the inability to reduce acute care episodes through better drug management. Because TRICARE covers outpatient prescription drugs, it may be that the savings potential for both Medicare and TRICARE is greater than in other case management programs.

Medicare Cost-Sharing for Medicare+Choice Enrollees

Medicare/DoD beneficiary enrollment in Medicare+Choice plans is likely to decline with the implementation of TFL and TRICARE Plus. Beneficiaries have little or no financial incentive to remain in a Medicare+Choice plan because they will have free choice of providers, no cost-sharing for Medicare-covered services, and prescription drug coverage. The liberal TFL benefits are coming at a time when many Medicare+Choice plans are offering fewer additional benefits at higher premiums. Medicare+Choice beneficiaries living in MTF catchment areas who have been using the MTFs for primary care will have an additional incentive to disenroll so that they will not be precluded from TRICARE Plus. Even though TFL beneficiaries have few financial incentives to enroll in Medicare+Choice, our interviews with DoD officials suggest that managed care may continue to attract beneficiaries who prefer an established network of providers and care management, prefer not to deal with fee-for-service paperwork, and do not have access to MTF care under TRICARE Plus.

National data on TFL beneficiary enrollment in Medicare+Choice plans and beneficiaries' use of MTF services are not available; however, data from the Senior Prime demonstration areas indicate that there has been significant usage of MTFs by Medicare+Choice enrollees in some areas (for example, before the demonstration, at least 20 percent of total inpatient days for dual eligibles at six sites were attributable to Medicare+Choice enrollees and were as high as 44 percent at Tacoma's Madigan Army Medical Center) (Farley et al., 1999). Allowing Medicare+Choice enrollees to use the MTF essentially results in double federal payment for the services: once for the Medicare per capita payment to the Medicare+ Choice plan and again for the MTF costs. Therefore, excluding Medicare+Choice enrollees from TRICARE Plus is likely to reduce total federal outlays.[5]

Medicare Partners (which was authorized but not implemented as part of the subvention demonstration) would have allowed Medicare+Choice organizations to contract with MTFs to provide services to Medicare-eligible DoD beneficiaries. Medicare policies ordinarily require that Medicare+Choice organizations contract only with Medicare-participating providers that furnish services to all Medicare beneficiaries. Because Medicare+Choice military enrollees have heretofore been able to obtain space-available care from MTFs at no cost to the Medicare+Choice organization, the managed care organizations have had little incentive to enter into agreements to pay for MTF services. If substantial Medicare+Choice enrollment continues in an area where there is MTF capacity, a cost-sharing arrangement between MTFs and Medicare+Choice organizations patterned after Medicare Partners might serve multiple purposes: increase the attractiveness of Medicare+Choice enrollment, eliminate duplicate payment, meet DoD readiness needs, and reduce MTF standby costs, particularly for specialty care.

The CMS has determined that Medicare+Choice organizations may enter into an agreement with DoD that will allow the Medicare+Choice organizations to design and market plans expressly for military retirees (Center for Medicare and Medicaid Services, 2001). For example, they could offer military retirees additional benefits or cost-sharing reductions that are the actuarial equivalents of pharmacy benefits offered to other Medicare beneficiaries (because military beneficiaries are already covered under TRICARE).

We assume that part of the attractiveness of marketing to military retirees within MTF catchment areas in the past has been the lower cost of civilian care for TFL beneficiaries using an MTF. Now that TRICARE Plus excludes Medicare+Choice enrollees, Medicare+Choice organizations may be less interested in marketing plans directed toward DoD retirees. However, the TRICARE Plus policy may also increase the willingness of Medicare+Choice organizations to participate in an arrangement such as Medicare Partners and pay for MTF care. In areas where the MTFs have the capacity to provide care to Medicare retirees, TRICARE Plus would expand the choices of TFL beneficiaries and could be beneficial to both the Medicare+Choice organizations and MTFs. It would enhance the marketing appeal of Medicare+Choice plans and, to the extent the negotiated rates are lower than civilian rates, reduce the costs for Medicare+Choice organizations that could be passed on to TFL beneficiaries through lesser cost-sharing and lower premiums. The MTFs would benefit if the negotiated rates exceeded the incremental costs of providing care to the Medicare+Choice enrollees.

---

[5] A recurring concern in establishing Medicare rates for Medicare+Choice plans has been lower Medicare fee-for-service expenditures resulting from use of MTF and DVA facilities. We believe that this is a separate issue and do not address it in this report.

Aligning Incentives at the MTF Level

Our descriptions of potential Medicare cost-sharing (or cost-savings) models have focused on the arrangement between the CMS and DoD that could be implemented through the accrual fund. TRICARE Senior Prime demonstrated the importance of aligning incentives for efficient care delivery at the MTF level. Careful attention would need to be paid to how and when DoD would distribute any Medicare payments for MTF services and how the costs of providing care to TFL beneficiaries are accounted for in the budgeting process. Unless funding for direct care services provided to TFL beneficiaries is structured to provide appropriate financial incentives to MTF managers, the opportunity for encouraging efficient care, with overall savings for the federal government, will be lost. Drawing on the experience of Senior Prime, consideration needs to be given to incentives that would

- encourage the provision of care to TFL beneficiaries without crowding out other military health system beneficiaries
- improve utilization management of MTF care
- manage referrals for civilian care.

Conclusions and Recommendations

The incentives under the current TFL program may not encourage the efficient delivery of services to TFL beneficiaries. In particular, there is an overall federal interest in DoD's continuing to provide direct care to TFL beneficiaries, assuming that the incremental costs of MTF care are less than the total costs of civilian care. Medicare cost-sharing for MTF care would foster viewing TFL beneficiaries as a joint responsibility of Medicare and DoD and lead to finding ways to provide those beneficiaries with the highest quality care at the least cost to the federal government. Cost-sharing also would provide DoD with financial resources to continue to provide direct care to TFL beneficiaries and has the potential to meet several policy goals: to allow TFL beneficiaries the choice between direct and civilian care, to serve DoD readiness needs, and most important, to provide high-quality health care services to TFL beneficiaries and the non-retiree military population at the least cost to the federal government. From the perspective of total federal outlays, however, a better understanding of how utilization by TFL beneficiaries who obtain care primarily from MTFs compares with utilization by TFL beneficiaries who obtain care solely through civilian providers is needed before policies are adopted that might encourage future expansion of MTF care for TFL beneficiaries.

We have described several options for joint Medicare-DoD sharing of the costs of direct care furnished to dual eligibles. These options provide a conceptual framework for discussions concerning potential Medicare cost-sharing arrangements. We recommend that additional research, using a combined Medicare/DoD database for TFL beneficiaries, be done to examine the cost implications of these options for DoD, the Medicare program, and total federal outlays. The following questions should be addressed in that additional research:

- How does the cost of direct care and civilian care for TFL beneficiaries compare, with respect to total cost, DoD cost, and Medicare cost, and by type of service (e.g., primary care, specialty care, pharmacy)?
- How does utilization by dual eligibles who mostly use MTFs compare with that of Medicare-eligible military retirees who mostly use civilian care? How does utilization by those dual eligibles compare with that of other Medicare beneficiaries?
- How do the Medicare per capita costs for dual eligibles compare with those of other Medicare beneficiaries? How do those costs for dual eligibles compare with the costs for dual eligibles before TFL?
- What are the marginal costs of providing MTF direct care to dual eligibles?
- How would payment rates based on Medicare payment methodologies compare with rates based on DoD rate schedules?
- What would be DoD's cost contribution based on the estimated current level of effort for Medicare fee-for-service beneficiaries? What would be DoD's cost contribution based on its fixed costs?
- What are the likely changes in the relative costs of TRICARE and Medicare for TFL beneficiaries over the next five to ten years under current policies? What are the likely changes in those relative costs under potential cost-sharing models?

The recommended research would provide the analyses that are needed to inform a policy discussion regarding appropriate cost-sharing arrangements between Medicare and DoD for TFL beneficiaries. In the end, the question of appropriate cost for direct care is likely to be answered through the political process, which should be informed by good information and analysis.

There are also similar cost-sharing issues for the Department of Veterans Affairs. In keeping with the notion of a "federal program" beneficiary, consideration should be given to expanding the recommended analyses to include veterans who are DoD retirees and/or Medicare beneficiaries and extending the discussions to include the DVA.

CHAPTER SIX

Conclusions and Recommendations

This study was undertaken in the months preceding implementation of the new TFL program on October 1, 2001. Given the limited time and resources for this study, we focused on three types of issue areas: those that DoD specifically asked us to examine, areas in which the Medicare and TRICARE benefits differ significantly, and areas of potential operational concern. Our goal was to identify issues that may pose policy and/or implementation problems. Where appropriate, we suggest policy options that DoD could consider in order to

- rationalize benefits by considering changes in the TFL benefit structure
- promote ease of operations by improving compatibility with Medicare benefits
- improve efficiency by promoting optimal use of direct care services and limiting excessive liability for civilian care
- improve the overall benefit package for Medicare-eligible military retirees.

As stated above, the initial work for this report was done prior to the implementation of TFL. Since the TFL implementation, we have not updated our report to include a discussion of actual experience under TFL or policy changes since the TFL implementation; however, we did update our discussion of certain issues, such as post-acute care service and behavioral health issues, which we had originally identified as being problematic and which have been addressed in subsequent legislation. We make note of those issues as well as those issues that remain potentially problematic in our conclusions that follow.

Benefit and Coverage Policies

Most health care services that are covered benefits under TRICARE are also covered benefits under Medicare, and vice versa. However, because TFL benefits are based on the existing TRICARE program, they were not expressly designed to fit together with Medicare benefits (in contrast to privately purchased Medicare supplemental or "Medigap" policies). As a result, there are benefit and coverage inconsistencies that pose operational challenges and that are likely to lead to confusion and misunderstanding for beneficiaries. The legislative changes in the FY2002 NDAA, which made TRICARE coverage and payment policies for SNF and HHA services conform with Medicare's policies, addressed the most problematic area. The changes in the FY2003 NDAA to eliminate the requirement for prior authorization for mental health inpatient hospital services and to provide that Medicare-approved providers are also approved to provide services under TFL should further reduce the administrative burden and confusion.

A potential concern regarding TFL is whether the coding specificity in Medicare's claims determination is sufficient for TRICARE to distinguish between Medicare coverage and medical necessity determinations, to establish its cost-sharing liability accurately, and to afford beneficiaries sufficient appeal rights. The issue of coding specificity is of particular concern for emerging technologies in which TRICARE and Medicare have differing coverage policies. We believe that TFL will highlight coverage inconsistencies between TRICARE and Medicare and may create pressure for consistent "federal" coverage policy. As a general rule, there should be a clear rationale for why a certain technology is covered by one program and not the other.

In addition, TMA is not represented on the CMS Medicare Coverage Advisory Committee. Coordination between the two programs could be enhanced if TMA became an active participant in the MCAC deliberations.

Recommendation: Claims for services for which Medicare and TRICARE coverage policies diverge should be reviewed to assure that the claims adjudication and appeals processes for TFL beneficiaries are working as intended.

Recommendation: TMA should participate in the CMS MCAC deliberations.

Although legislation subsequent to this study improved coordination of benefits between Medicare and TRICARE for post-acute care services and behavioral health services, some potential issues remain. For post-acute care services, the potential concern is the lack of any limitation on the duration of SNF benefits and whether there should be any TFL enhancements for HHA care. For the first 100 days of SNF care, TFL beneficiaries have no cost-sharing liabilities and, as a result, no financial incentives to seek care through less-costly alternatives. After 100 days, when there is 25 percent cost-sharing with TRICARE, TFL beneficiaries have some incentive to find alternative care settings. However, with home health care limited to part-time and intermittent care, some beneficiaries with skilled nursing needs may find continuing SNF care an attractive option.

Recommendation: The use of post-acute care services by TFL beneficiaries should be monitored. Particular attention should be paid to beneficiaries with continued SNF stays after their Medicare SNF benefits have been exhausted. If there is a significant incidence of continued SNF stays, a study of the cost effectiveness of expanded home health benefits would be warranted.

Differences in Medicare and TRICARE coverage policies for behavioral health services create complex issues in implementing TFL. These differences make it likely that beneficiaries will find this area of their health coverage relatively confusing, even with the TRICARE preauthorization requirement for inpatient psychiatric care covered by Medicare Part A benefits, which became effective October 1, 2003.

TRICARE's lifetime limit of three benefit periods for the coverage of substance abuse treatment services also may remain problematic. Because TRICARE and Medicare define benefit periods differently, the determination of when and how the TRICARE limit is reached is likely to be somewhat difficult and confusing to both providers and beneficiaries. With regard to outpatient mental health services, TFL beneficiaries have unlimited access to medically necessary psychiatric treatment and few financial incentives to limit that care.

Recommendation: DoD should examine and consider the impact of removing the three-benefit-period limit on substance abuse benefits for the TFL population.

Recommendation: DoD should conduct a close examination of mental health service utilization and costs to determine the impact of covering outpatient mental health without cost-sharing or benefit limits.

TFL Beneficiary Cost-Sharing for Civilian Care

TFL is being implemented without premiums, deductibles, or copayments. Compared with the health insurance options previously available to Medicare-eligible military retirees, TFL is likely to be of substantially greater value to most beneficiaries. At the same time, TFL will substantially increase federal spending due to the new benefits per se and because the absence of cost-sharing is likely to increase health care use because beneficiaries no longer have cost-sharing as an incentive to use care efficiently.

Both DoD and Medicare are likely to benefit if modest cost-sharing is introduced into TFL—for instance, such as the cost-sharing that military retirees under age 65 currently have under TRICARE Prime. For Medicare beneficiaries, supplemental coverage with modest cost-sharing substantially reduces the out-of-pocket costs that would arise under the standard Medicare benefit, while retaining some modest incentives to control health care use and costs.

The introduction of cost-sharing in TFL would likely serve to reduce the cost of the program to the federal government, all else being equal. However, this change could be made revenue-neutral by applying the resulting savings toward other benefits for the covered population—such as enhanced post-acute or long-term care coverage or a reduction in the current TFL out-of-pocket maximum—thereby potentially increasing the overall value of the TFL benefit.

Recommendation: DoD should consider introducing modest cost-sharing in TFL for civilian care. Further research into the preferences of TFL beneficiaries and the likely consequences of introducing cost-sharing (versus continued free care) for TFL would help to identify strategies to maximize the overall value of the TFL benefit.

Managing MTF Care Provided to TFL Beneficiaries

Relatively little opportunity exists to implement managed care practices under standard Medicare and TFL. However, given the apparent desire of many TFL beneficiaries to receive care from military providers, DoD may have the opportunity to provide managed care for some elderly beneficiaries via programs instituted at MTFs, such as TRICARE Plus.

We think it is likely that TRICARE Plus and similar programs will be well received by beneficiaries, especially because participation in those programs is voluntary. We also think it is plausible that such programs could improve clinical outcomes for some enrollees, relative to both standard Medicare and the current space-available policy. However, the scope of such improvements depends critically on how and for whom care management programs are implemented. DoD may be able to increase the likelihood of improved clinical outcomes by targeting TRICARE Plus enrollment to patients who are likely to benefit from primary care management and implementing effective care management programs for those patients. Because DoD must assume full responsibility for the cost of care provided to Medicare-eligible beneficiaries at MTFs, DoD's patient care costs are almost certainly higher under TRICARE Plus than the costs of care provided under Medicare. On the other hand, treating Medicare-eligible beneficiaries in MTFs helps DoD to fulfill its readiness mission. How these factors balance on net is unknown.

Recommendation: Further research regarding the effects of MTF primary care management on patient outcomes and treatment costs, and regarding providers' case-mix preferences and the relationship between primary care management and readiness, should be conducted. Such research could determine the overall cost-effectiveness of TRICARE Plus from the perspective of DoD and the federal government, relative to alternative models for care management and readiness training.

Models for Medicare's Sharing in MTF Costs

DoD's new obligations for TFL beneficiaries raise issues related to the cost of furnishing direct care relative to making secondary payments for civilian care. These new obligations also raise the issue of whether Medicare should share in the costs of direct care services now that the traditional division of responsibility for military retiree health care costs no longer exists.

There is an overall federal interest in DoD's continuing to provide direct care to TFL beneficiaries, assuming that the incremental costs of MTF care are less than the total costs of civilian care. Medicare cost-sharing for MTF care would foster viewing TFL beneficiaries as a joint responsibility of Medicare DoD and lead to finding ways to provide those beneficiaries with the highest-quality care at the least cost to the federal government. Cost-sharing also would provide DoD with the financial resources to continue to provide direct care to TFL beneficiaries and has the potential to meet several policy goals: to allow TFL beneficiary choice between direct and civilian care, to serve DoD readiness needs, and most important, to provide high-quality health care services to TFL beneficiaries and the non-retiree military population at the least cost to the federal government. From the perspective of total federal outlays, however, a better understanding of how utilization by TFL beneficiaries who obtain care primarily from MTFs compares with utilization by TFL beneficiaries who obtain care solely through civilian providers is needed before policies are adopted that might encourage future expansion of MTF care for TFL beneficiaries.

Recommendation: Additional research, using a combined Medicare/DoD database for TFL beneficiaries, should be conducted to determine the cost implications of potential cost-sharing options for DoD, the Medicare program, and total federal outlays. This additional research would provide the analyses that are needed to inform a policy discussion regarding appropriate cost-sharing arrangements between Medicare and DoD for TFL beneficiaries.

In the end, the question of appropriate costs for direct care is likely to be answered through the political process, which should be supported by good information and analysis. There are also are similar cost-sharing issues for the Department of Veterans Affairs. In keeping with the notion of a "federal program" beneficiary, consideration should be given to expanding the recommended analyses to include veterans who are DoD retirees and/or Medicare beneficiaries and extending the discussions to include the DVA.

Bibliography

Administration on Aging, *America's Families Care: A Report on the Needs of America's Family Caregivers,* Washington, D.C.: Administration on Aging, U.S. Department of Health and Human Services, 2000.

American Association of Retired People, "Out-of-Pocket Spending on Health Care by Medicare Beneficiaries Age 65 and Older: 1999 Projections," Washington, D.C.: AARP Public Policy Institute, December 1999 (http://research.aarp.org/health/listchron.html; last accessed July 2004).

Assistant Secretary for Planning and Evaluation and Administration on Aging, *Informal Caregiving: Compassion in Action*, Washington, D.C.: Department of Health and Human Services, 1998.

Aubert, R. E., W. H. Herman, J. Waters, W. Moore, D. Sutton, B. L. Peterson, C. M. Bailey, and J. P. Koplan, "Nurse Case Management to Improve Glycemic Control in Diabetic Patients in a Health Maintenance Organization: A Randomized, Controlled Trial," *Annals of Internal Medicine,* Vol. 129, No. 8, 1998, pp. 605–612.

Beck, A., et al., "A Randomized Trial of Group Outpatient Visits for Chronically Ill Older HMO Members: The Cooperative Health Care Clinic," *Journal of the American Geriatrics Society,* Vol. 45, 1997, pp. 543–549.

Boult, C., J. Rassen, A. Rassen, B. J. Moore, and S. Bouquillon, "The Effect of Case Management on the Costs of Health Care for Enrollees in Medicare HMOs," *Journal of the American Geriatrics Society,* Vol. 48, 2000a, pp. 996–1001.

Boult, C., J. Rassen, A. Rassen, B. J. Moore, and S. Robison, "The Effect of Case Management on the Costs of Health Care for Enrollees in Medicare Plus Choice Plans: A Randomized Trial, *Journal of the American Geriatrics Society,* Vol. 48, No. 8, 2000b, pp. 996–1001.

Broadhead, E. W., D. G. Blazer, and L. K. George, "Depression, Disability Days, and Days Lost from Work in a Prospective Epidemiologic Survey," *Journal of the American Medical Association,* Vol. 264, 1990, pp. 2524–2528.

Brook, R. H., et al., "Does Free Care Improve Adults' Health? Results from a Randomized Controlled Trial," *New England Journal of Medicine,* Vol. 309, 1983, pp. 1426–1434.

Brook, R. H., et al., *The Effect of Coinsurance on the Health of Adults,* Santa Monica, Calif.: RAND Corporation, R-3055-HHS, 1984.

Callahan, C. M., S. L. Hui, N. A. Nienaber, B. S. Musick, and W. M. Tierney, "Longitudinal Study of Depression and Health Services Use Among Elderly Primary Care Patients," *Journal of the American Geriatrics Society,* Vol. 42, 1997, pp. 833–838.

Caplan, G. A., J. A. Ward, N. J. Brennan, J. Coconis, N. Board, and A. Brown, "Hospital in the Home: A Randomized Controlled Trial," *The Medical Journal of Australia,* Vol. 170, 1999, pp. 156–160.

Center for Medicare and Medicaid Services, "Information on Employer-Only Plans for Military Retirees," September 16, 2001 (www.hcfa.gov/medicare/empgrp.htm; last accessed October 2001).

Coronel, S., *Long Term Care Insurance in 1996*, Washington, D.C.: Health Insurance Association of America, September 1998.

Coughlin, T., K. Liu, and T. D. McBride, "Severely Disabled Elderly Persons with Catastrophic Health Expenses: Sources and Determinants," *Gerontologist*, Vol. 32, June 1992, pp. 391–403.

Cummings, J. E., et al., "Cost-Effectiveness of Veterans Administration Hospital-Based Home Care: A Randomized Controlled Trial," *Archives of Internal Medicine*, Vol. 150, 1990, pp. 1274–1280.

Curley, C., J. E. McEachern, and T. Speroff, "A Firm Trial of Interdisciplinary Rounds on the Inpatient Medical Wards: An Intervention Designed Using Continuous Quality Improvement," *Medical Care*, Vol. 36, No. 8 (Supp.), 1998, pp. AS4–12.

Department of Defense, Assistant Secretary of Defense, Health Affairs, *2002 TRICARE Stakeholder's Report: Our Promises Kept, Our Nation Calls*, 2002 (http://tricare.osd.mil/stakeholders/default.cfm; last accessed July 2004).

Department of Veterans Affairs, *FY2002 Annual Accountability Report Statistical Appendix*, 2002 (http://www.va.gov/vetdata/ProgramStatics/index.htm; last accessed July 2004).

Deputy Secretary of Defense, "Strengthening the Medical Functions of the Department of Defense," memorandum, October 1, 1991.

Farley, D. O., D. P. Goldman, G. M. Careter, L. M. Davis, J. B. Carleton, G. K. Cherry, D. A. Freund, and T. C. Rowe, *Interim Report: Evaluation of the Medicare-DoD Subvention Demonstration*, Santa Monica, Calif.: RAND Corporation, MR-1106.0-HCFA, July 1999.

Farley, D. O., K. M. Harris, J. S. Ashwood, G. J. Dydek, and J. B. Carelton, *The First Year of the Medicare-DoD Subvention Demonstration: Evaluation Report for 1999*, Santa Monica, Calif.: RAND Corporation, MR-1271.0-HCFA, December 2000.

Farley, D. O., K. M. Harris, L. M. Davis, J. S. Ashwood, G. K. Cherry, G. J. Dydek, and J. B. Carleton, *Evaluation of the Medicare-DoD Subvention Demonstration: Final Report*, Santa Monica, Calif.: RAND Corporation, MR-1580-CMS, 2003.

Feder, J., H. L. Kosimar, and M. Niefeld, "Long Term Care in the United States: An Overview," *Health Affairs*, May/June 2000, Vol. 19, No. 4, pp. 40–55.

Federal Register, April 27, 1999 (64 FR 22619-22625).

Fleming, M. F., K. L. Barry, L. B. Manwell, K. Johnson, and R. London, "Brief Physician Advice for Problem Drinkers: A Randomized Controlled Trial in Community-Based Primary Care Practices," *Journal of the American Medical Association*, Vol. 277, No. 13, 1997, pp. 1039–1045.

Fleming, M. F., and L. B. Manwell, "Brief Intervention in Primary Care Setting," *Alcohol Research and Health*, Vol. 23, No. 2, 1999, pp. 128–137.

Gagnon, A. J., G. Schein, L. McVey, and H. Bergman, "A Randomized Controlled Trial of Nurse Case Management of Frail Older People," *Journal of the American Geriatrics Society*, Vol. 47, 1999, pp. 1118–1124.

Gallo, J. J., P. V. Rabins, and S. Illiffe, "The 'Research Magnificent' in Late Life; Psychiatric Epidemiology and the Primary Health Care of Older Adults," *International Journal of Psychiatry Medicine*, Vol. 27, 1997, pp. 185–204.

Gemignani, J., "Zeroing in on Costly Chronic Disease," *Business and Health*, Vol. 16, No. 2, 1998, pp. 47–48.

German, P. S., S. Shapiro, and E. A. Skinner, "Mental Health of the Elderly: Use of Health and Mental Health Services," *Journal of the American Geriatric Society*, Vol. 33, 1985, pp. 246–252.

Glasgow, R. E., C.P.A. La, D. J. Toobert, J. Brown, S. E. Hampson, and M. C. Riddle, "Long-Term Effects and Costs of Brief Behavioural Dietary Intervention for Patients with Diabetes Delivered from the Medical Office, *Patient Education & Counseling*, Vol. 32, No. 3, 1997, pp. 175–184.

Gold, M. R., J. E. Siegel, L. B. Russell, and M. C. Weinstein, eds., *Cost-Effectiveness in Health and Medicine*, New York: Oxford University Press, 1996.

Grossman, J. M., et al., "Reversal of Fortune: Medicare+Choice Collides with Market Forces," Washington, D.C.: Center for Studying Health System Change, Issue Brief No. 52, 2002.

Health Care Financing Administration, *Medicare and Your Mental Health Benefits*, Baltimore, Md.: U.S Department of Human Services, 2000.

Health Care Financing Administration, "Medicare Coverage Policy: Clinical Trials; Final National Coverage Policy Determination," September 16, 2001a (www.hcfa.gov/coverage/8d2.htm; last accessed September 2001).

Health Care Financing Administration, "Medicare Coverage Policy: Clinical Trials; Provider Bulletin," September 16, 2001b (www.hcfa.gov/coverage/8d2.htm; last accessed September 2001).

Heidenreich, P. A., C. M. Ruggerio, and B. M. Massie, "Effect of a Home Monitoring System on Hospitalization and Resource Use for Patients with Heart Failure," *American Heart Journal*, Vol. 138, No. 4, Part 1, 1999, pp. 633–640.

Henessey, K. D., and H. H. Goldman, "Full Parity: Steps Toward Treatment Equity for Mental and Addictive Disorders," *Health Affairs*, Vol. 20, No. 4, 2001, pp. 58–67.

Himelhoch, S., et al., "Chronic Medical Illness, Depression, and Use of Acute Medical Services Among Medicare Beneficiaries," *Medical Care*, Vol. 42, No. 6, June 2004, pp. 512–521.

Hosek, S. D., B. W. Bennett, J. L. Buchanan, M. S. Marquis, K. A. McGuigan, J. M. Hanley, R. Madison, A. Rastegar, and J. Hawes-Dawson, *The Demand for Military Health Care: Supporting Research for Comprehensive Study of the Military Health-Care System*, Santa Monica, Calif.: RAND Corporation, MR-407-1-OSD, 1995.

Jeste, D. V., G. S. Alexopoulous, S. J. Bartels, J. L. Cummings, J. L. Gallo, G. L. Gottlieb, M. C. Halpain, B. W. Palmer, T. L. Patterson, C. F. Reynolds, and B. D. Lebowitz, "Consensus Statement on the Upcoming Crisis in Geriatric Mental Health," *Archives of General Psychiatry*, Vol. 56, 1999, pp. 848–853.

Kaiser Family Foundation, *How Medicare HMO Withdrawals Affect Beneficiary Benefits, Costs, and Continuity of Care*, Menlo Park: Calif.: Kaiser Family Foundation, 1999.

Kaiser Family Foundation, *Medicare at a Glance*, Menlo Park, Calif.: Kaiser Family Foundation, 2001.

Kaiser Family Foundation, *Erosion of Private Health Insurance Coverage for Retirees: Findings from the 2000 and 2001 Retiree Health and Prescription Drug Coverage Survey*, Menlo Park, Calif.: Kaiser Family Foundation, 2002.

Kane, R. L., R. A. Kane, M. Finch, C. Harrington, R. Newcomer, N. Miller, and M. Hulbert, "S/HMOs, The Second Generation: Building on the Experience of the First Social Health Maintenance Organization Demonstrations," *Journal of the American Geriatrics Society*, Vol. 45, 1997, pp. 1010–1017.

Kemper, P., R. Applebaum, and M. Harrigan, "Community Care Demonstrations: What Have We Learned?" *Health Care Financing Review*, Vol. 8, 1987, pp. 87–100.

Klerman, J. A., and M. R. Kilburn, *The Effects of Changing the Staffing in Military Treatment Facilities,* Santa Monica, Calif.: RAND Corporation, MR-631-OSD, 1998.

Laschober, M. A., et al., "Trends in Medicare Supplemental Insurance and Prescription Drug Coverage, 1996–1999," *Health Affairs (Web Exclusives),* February 27, 2002, pp. w127–w138.

Levy, R. A., and R. D. Miller, "Options for Improving Access to Health Care for Retirees," Alexandria, Va.: Center for Naval Analyses, CAB 98-60, September 1998 (http://www.cna.org/research/pdfs/health/cab98_60.pdf, last accessed April 2004).

Liu, K., K. G. Manton, and C. Aragon, *Changes in Home Care Use by Older People with Disabilities: 1982–1994,* Washington, D.C.: AARP Policy Institute, January 2000.

"Long-Term Care Insurance Special Report: How Will You Pay for Your Old Age?" *Consumer Reports,* October 1997, pp. 36–50.

Lorig, K. R., D. S. Sobel, A. L. Stewart, B. W. Brown, Jr., A. Bandura, P. Ritter, V. M. Gonzalez, D. D. Laurent, and H. R. Holman, "Evidence Suggesting That a Chronic Disease Self-Management Program Can Improve Health Status While Reducing Hospitalization: A Randomized Trial," *Medical Care,* Vol. 37, 1999, pp. 5–14.

Lutzky, S., J. Corea, L. Alecxih, L. Marburger, and K. Wee, *Preliminary Data from a Survey of Employers Offering Group Long Term Care Insurance to Their Employees: Interim Report,* prepared by the Lewin Group for the Department of Health and Human Services, Office of Disability, Aging, and Long-Term Care, 1999.

Manning, W. G., J. P. Newhouse, N. Duan, E. B. Keeler, and A. Leibowitz, "Health Insurance and the Demand for Medical Care: Evidence from a Randomized Experiment," *American Economic Review,* Vol. 77, No. 3, 1987, pp. 251–277.

McCulloch, D. K., M. J. Price, M. Hindmarsh, and E. H. Wagner, "A Population-Based Approach to Diabetes Management in a Primary Care Setting: Early Results and Lessons Learned," *Effective Clinical Practice,* Vol. 1, No. 1, 1998, pp. 12–22.

Medicare Fact Sheet, Health Care Financing Administration, January 19, 2001 (www.hcfa.gov; last accessed August 2001).

National Alliance for Caregiving/National Center on Women and Aging, Brandeis University, *The MetLife Juggling Acts Study: Balancing Caregiving with Work and the Costs Involved*, New York: Metropolitan Life Insurance Company, 1999.

Naylor, M. D., D. Brooten, R. Campbell, B. S. Jacobsen, M. D. Mezey, M. V. Pauly, and J. S. Schwartz, "Comprehensive Discharge Planning and Home Follow-up of Hospitalized Elders: A Randomized Clinical Trial," *Journal of the American Medical Association,* Vol. 281, No. 7, 1999, pp. 613–620.

Newhouse, J. P., and the Insurance Experiment Group, *Free For All,* Cambridge, Mass.: Harvard University Press, 1993.

Office of Personnel Management, *Federal Long Term Care Insurance Program (FLTCIP),* "Frequently Asked Questions" (http://www.opm.gov/insure/ltc/; last accessed April 2004).

Olfson, M., and H. A. Pincus, "Measuring Outpatient Mental Health Care in the United States," *Health Affairs,* Winter 1994, pp. 172–180.

Peele, P. B., "Benefit Limits in Managed Behavioral Health Care: Do They Matter?" *Journal of Behavioral Health Services and Research*, Vol. 26, No. 4, 1999, p. 438.

Philbin, E. F., "Comprehensive Multidisciplinary Programs for the Management of Patients with Congestive Heart Failure," *Journal of General Internal Medicine,* Vol. 14, No. 2, 1999, pp. 130–135.

Renders, C. M., G. D. Valk, S. Griffin, E. H. Wagner, J. T. Eijk, and W.J.J. Assendelft, "Interventions to Improve the Management of Diabetes Mellitus in Primary Care, Outpatient and Community Settings," *Cochrane Review,* The Cochrane Library, Issue 2, 2001.

The Retired Officers Association, "Legislative Initiatives: Frequently Asked Questions About the Government Sponsored Long-Term Care Group Plan," May 2001.

Rice, B., "Keep Close Tabs on Your Chronic Disease Patients, *Medical Economics,* Vol. 77, No. 22, 2000, pp. 81–84, 89–90.

Rich, M. W., "Heart Failure Disease Management: A Critical Review," *Journal of Cardiac Failure,* Vol. 5, No. 1, 1999, pp. 64–75.

Rich, M. W., V. Beckham, C. Wittenberg, C. L. Leven, K. E. Freedland, and R. M. Carney, "A Multidisciplinary Intervention to Prevent the Readmission of Elderly Patients with Congestive Heart Failure," *New England Journal of Medicine,* Vol. 333, No. 18, 1995, pp. 1190–1195.

Rich, M. W., and R. F. Nease, "Cost-Effectiveness Analysis in Clinical Practice: The Case of Heart Failure," *Archives of Internal Medicine,* Vol. 159, No. 15, 1999, pp. 1690–1700.

Ringel, J. S., S. D. Hosek, B. A. Vollaard, and S. Mahnovski, *The Elasticity of Demand for Health Care: A Review of the Literature and Its Application to the Military Health System,* Santa Monica, Calif.: RAND Corporation, MR-1355, 2002.

Robins, L. N., and D. A. Regier, *Psychiatric Disorders in America: The Epidemiologic Catchment Area Study,* New York: The Free Press, 1991.

Rudy, E. B., B. J. Daly, S. Douglas, H. D. Montenegro, R. Song, and M. A. Dyer, "Patient Outcomes for the Chronically Critically Ill: Special Care Unit Versus Intensive Care Unit," *Nursing Research,* Vol. 44, No. 6, 1995, pp. 324–331.

Schoenbaum, M., et al., "The Cost-Effectiveness of Practice-Initiated Quality Improvement for Depression: Results from a Randomized, Controlled Trial," *Journal of the American Medical Association,* Vol. 286, No. 11, 2001, pp. 1325–1330.

Schoenbaum, M., K. Harris, G. Cecchine, A. Suarez, C. Horn, and C. R. Anthony, *Final Evaluation Report for TRICARE Senior Supplement Demonstration Program,* Santa Monica, Calif.: RAND Corporation, MR-1459-OSD, 2002.

Simon, G. E., M. vonKorff, and W. Barlow, "Health Care Costs of Primary Care Patients with Recognized Depression, *Archives of General Psychiatry,* Vol. 52, 1995, pp. 850–856.

Stessman, J., et al., "Decreased Hospital Utilization by Older Adults Attributable to a Home Hospitalization Program," *Journal of the American Geriatrics Society,* Vol. 44, 1996, pp. 591–598.

Sturm, R., "How Expensive Is Unlimited Mental Health Care Coverage Under Managed Care?" *Journal of the American Medical Association,* Vol. 278, No. 18, 1997, pp. 1533–1537.

Sturm, R., et al., "How Expensive Are Unlimited Substance Abuse Benefits Under Managed Care?" *Journal of Behavioral Health Services and Research,* Vol. 26, No. 2, 1999, pp. 203–210.

Substance Abuse and Mental Health Services Administration (SAMHSA) and the National Institutes of Health, *Mental Health: A Report of the Surgeon General 1999,* U.S. Department of Health and Human Services, Office of the Surgeon General, SAMHSA (http://www.mentalhealth.samhsa. gov/cmhs/surgeongeneral/surgeongeneralrpt.asp; last accessed July 2004).

TRICARE Management Activity, "Health Care Survey of DoD Beneficiaries," Falls Church, Va., n.d. (http://www.tricare.osd.mil/survey/hcsurvey/default.htm; last accessed July 2004).

TRICARE Management Activity, *TRICARE/CHAMPUS Policy Manual 6010.47-M,* June 25, 1999 (updated version available at http://www.tricare.osd.mil/tricaremanuals/; last accessed April 2004).

TRICARE Management Activity, operations staff, personal communication, Aurora, Colo., July 25, 2001a.

TRICARE Management Activity, staff presentation, "Desire to Use MTFs by the Over-65 Population Under NDAA01: Early Survey Results," Falls Church, Va., 2001b.

TRICARE Management Activity, *TRICARE Reimbursement Manual 6010.53M,* March 15, 2002a (http://www.tricare.osd.mil/tricaremanuals/; last accessed April 2004).

TRICARE Management Activity, Resource Management Directive, "The DoD Medicare Eligible Retiree Health Care Fund (the 'Accrual Fund')," briefing slides, September 26, 2002b (http://www.tricare.osd.mil/ebc/rm_home/files/fa/fa_accrual_26sept02_update.ppt; last accessed April 2004).

Unutzer, J., et al., "Depressive Symptoms and the Cost of Health Services in HMO Patients Age 65 Years and Older," *Journal of the American Medical Association,* Vol. 277, 1997, pp. 1618–1623.

U.S. Census Bureau, "Table 1. Median Value of Assets for Households, by Type of Asset Owned and Selected Characteristics: 1995," *Asset Ownership of Households: 1995,* 1995 (www.census.gov/hhes/www/wealth/1995/wlth95-1.html; last accessed April 2004).

U.S. Census Bureau, "Table A. Comparison of Summary Measures of Income by Selected Characteristics: 1989, 1998, and 1999," *Income 1999,* 1999 (www.census.gov/hhes/income/income99/99tablea.html; last accessed April 2004).

U.S. Congressional Budget Office, *Reducing the Deficit: Spending and Revenue Options,* March 1997 (ftp://ftp.cbo.gov/0xx/doc6/chapt2.pdf, last accessed July 2004).

U.S. Congressional Budget Office, *Budget Options for National Defense,* March 2000 (ftp://ftp.cbo.gov/18xx/doc1873/ndv2000.pdf, last accessed July 2004).

U.S. Department of Health and Human Services, *Mental Health: A Report of the Surgeon General,* Rockville, Md.: U.S. Department of Health and Human Services, Substance Abuse and Mental Health Services Administration, Center for Mental Health Services, National Institutes of Health, National Institute of Mental Health, 1999 (http://mentalhealth.samhsa.gov/features/surgeongeneralreport/home.asp; last accessed July 2004).

U.S. General Accounting Office, *Medigap Insurance: Plans Are Widely Available but Have Limited Benefits and May Have High Costs,* Washington, D.C.: GAO, GAO-01-941, 2001a.

U.S. General Accounting Office, *Retiree Health Insurance: Gaps in Coverage and Availability,* Washington, D.C.: GAO, GAO-02-178T, 2001b.

U.S. General Accounting Office, *Medicare Subvention Demonstration: Greater Access Improved Enrollee Satisfaction but Raised DOD Costs,* Washington, D.C.: GAO,GAO-02-68, October 31, 2001c.

U.S. General Accounting Office, *Medicare Subvention Demonstration: DoD Costs and Medicare Spending,* Washington, D.C.: GAO, GAO-02-67, October 31, 2001d.

U.S. General Accounting Office, *Medicare Subvention Demonstration: Pilot Satisfies Enrollees, Raises Cost and Management Issues for DOD Health Care,* Washington, D.C.: GAO, GAO-02-284, February 11, 2002.

Wagner, D. L., *Comparative Analysis of Caregiver Data for Caregivers to the Elderly: 1987 and 1997,* Bethesda, Md.: National Alliance for Caregiving, 1997.

Weiss Ratings, *Prescription Drug Costs Boost Medigap Premiums Dramatically,* Palm Beach Gardens, Fla.: Weiss Ratings, 2000.

Weissert, W. G., C. M. Cready, and J. E. Pawelak, "The Past and Future of Home and Community-Based Long-Term Care," *The Milbank Quarterly,* Vol. 66, 1988, pp. 309–388.

Wells, K. B., et al., "Impact of Disseminating Quality Improvement Programs for Depression in Managed Primary Care: Results from a Randomized Controlled Trial," *Journal of the American Medical Association,* Vol. 283, No. 2, 2000, pp. 212–220.

Wiener, J. L., et al., *Sharing the Burden: Strategies for Public and Private Long-Term Care Insurance,* Washington, D.C.: The Brookings Institution, 2000.